JOHANNA BEYER

I0879457

AMERICAN

Composers

A list of books in the series appears
at the end of this book.

Johanna Beyer

Amy C. Beal

UNIVERSITY OF ILLINOIS PRESS
Urbana, Chicago, and Springfield

Publication of this book is supported by the Bukofzer Endowment of the American Musicological Society, funded in part by the National Endowment for the Humanities and the Andrew W. Mellon Foundation.

© 2015 by the Board of Trustees of the University of Illinois
All rights reserved
Manufactured in the United States of America
1 2 3 4 5 C P 5 4 3 2 1
∞ This book is printed on acid-free paper.

Library of Congress Cataloging-in-Publication Data
Beal, Amy C.
Johanna Beyer / by Amy C. Beal.
pages cm.—(American composers)
Includes bibliographical references and index.
ISBN 978-0-252-03915-7 (hardcover : alk. paper) —
ISBN 978-0-252-08072-2 (pbk. : alk. paper) —
ISBN 978-0-252-09713-3 (e-book)
1. Beyer, Johanna Magdalena, 1888–1944.
2. Composers—United States—Biography.
3. Beyer, Johanna Magdalena, 1888–1944 —
Criticism and interpretation. I. Title.
ML410.B58562B43 2015
780.92—dc23 2014036351
[B]

for Larry

CONTENTS

ACKNOWLEDGMENTS

I AM GRATEFUL TO ALL THE PEOPLE who have shared this research journey with me and who have helped me in various ways, including Charles Amirkhanian, Bettina Aptheker, Jay Arms, Dennis Bathory-Kitsz, Sally Bick, George Boziwick, William Brooks, Rich Capen, Mary Jane Cope, Ron Coulter, Rory Cowal, Gary Galván, Sarah Gerk, Ralph Roger Glöckler, Julie Hanify, Michael Hicks, Ken Hullican, Jennifer DeLapp, Cordula Jaspar, John Kennedy, Maryann LaBella, Rachel Lumsden, Gayle Sherwood Magee, Katie Clare Mazzeo, Gordon Mumma, Dard Neuman, Kathleen Nutter, Tanya Pearson, Robin Preiss, Nancy Rao, Herbert Reynolds, John Shepard, Christopher Shultis, Thomas Smetryns, Ann Snitow, John Spilker, Paul Tai, Jeffrey Taylor, Kent Underwood, Carole Vance, William Winant, and all the wonderful performers in the all-Beyer concert at the University of California, Santa Cruz (UCSC), held May 1, 2013.

I am indebted to Editor-in-Chief Laurie Matheson at the University of Illinois Press for her committed advocacy for this—perhaps somewhat unusual—addition to the American Composers series. I wish also to thank the readers of both the book proposal and the finished manuscript. In particular, I deeply appreciate an anonymous reader's and Melissa J. de Graaf's detailed commentary and thoughtful suggestions for revisions that have made the final product better than it would have been otherwise. I am also particularly grateful for the generosity of time and patience Mark Davidson offered in helping prepare the score examples and photographic images reproduced here. This research has been supported by UCSC Arts Research Institute and Committee on Research grants.

My work on Beyer began during fall 2006 as daily trips to Princeton University's Firestone Library atrium for the arduous task of hand copying Beyer's confusing *Cluster Suite*, and continued the following spring with weekly trips to the New

York Public Library's Music Division at Lincoln Center for the transcription of Beyer's letters to Henry Cowell. Now, finished at last, this book is dedicated to Larry Polansky, who has worked altruistically to make this neglected composer's work available to the world. His passion and patience have inspired me to persevere through many moments of doubt about my ability ever to complete this project, given all its dead ends and confounding mysteries.

JOHANNA BEYER

Introduction

From Leipzig to the Bronx

> I write music because I love to write music.
> I have to! It is an inner urge. It is a necessity.
> —JOHANNA BEYER, Composers' Forum-Laboratory, May 19, 1937

> Most of her pieces have apparently never been performed, and she remains a real enigma.
> We hope to correct that a bit this year.
> —Letter from John Kennedy to Nicolas Slonimsky, January 24, 1988

IN JANUARY 2013, while researching independent American music publishing in the Peter Garland Papers held by the Harry Ransom Center at the University of Texas in Austin, I unexpectedly came across several references to the composer Johanna Beyer:

> Who is this lady, Johanna Beyer? I haven't been able to find anything out about her yet. I've been looking in the more obscure places, but to no avail. (Letter from Michael Byron to Peter Garland, November 28, 1973)

> A brief question, about Joanna [*sic*] Beyer. Have you found any further biographical information about her, other than that she was born in Leipzig in 1888 and died, apparently in 1944? Charles Amirkhanian hasn't found much more, nor have I had much luck. (Letter from Gordon Mumma to Peter Garland, September 8, 1980)

> Right now we have this cooperative Beyer edition project going on [. . .]. This is fun: about 10 of the scores are out now being copied, and we'll bring 'em out one at a time until some miracle happens and we get some money to publish 'em. (Letter from Larry Polansky to Peter Garland, September 8, 1994)

> I'm enclosing a copy of the new Beyer article in [*Musical Quarterly*]. . . . We've done 10 editions now and I'm kind of hoping I can stop working on her (I think she's a hoax anyway). (Letter from Larry Polansky to Peter Garland, June 25, 1997)

At the time of this writing, some forty years after Michael Byron first posed the question, we are still asking: "Who is this lady, Johanna Beyer?" Some basic facts of her life are now known. But Polansky's tongue-in-cheek remark that he "think[s] she's a hoax" points to the enduring mystery of this prolific yet elusive composer.

Johanna Magdalena Beyer was born in Leipzig on July 11, 1888. Very little is known about her early life. We know a number of addresses in Germany between 1905 and 1915, and that she made at least seven transatlantic passages between 1911 and 1935.[1] She first lived in New York from April 1911 until June 1914, but we know neither what she did there during those years nor what she did in Germany during World War I. According to a curriculum vitae Beyer seems to have created around 1937 (hereinafter: 1937 CV), we know that back in Germany, she sang for three years in the Leipziger Singakademie and graduated from a German music conservatory in September 1923.[2] She returned to New York on November 14, 1923. Her departure from Germany coincided roughly with the so-called "Beer Hall Putsch"—Adolf Hitler's failed attempt to overthrow the German government—in Munich, November 8–9, 1923.

Beyer's re-arrival in the United States in late 1923 coincided with an exciting year for music in New York City. In February 1924, young pianist Henry Cowell gave his Carnegie Hall debut concert; the Paul Whiteman Orchestra premiered George Gershwin's *Rhapsody in Blue* a week later; Aaron Copland returned to New York after three years in France and began teaching at the New School for Social Research; and in October, Louis Armstrong joined the Fletcher Henderson Orchestra at the Roseland Ballroom. By 1924, Blanche Walton's apartment at Central Park West and West 68th Street had become a popular meeting place for modernist musicians; one year later Cowell and Ruth Crawford met in Chicago. The year 1924, not to mention the rest of the Roaring Twenties in New York City, must have been eye-opening for an ambitious music student like Beyer who had been born during the same decade as Béla Bartók, Alban Berg, and Igor Stravinsky. In the years following her arrival in New York, Beyer earned two degrees from the Mannes School of Music, and she took additional classes at Mannes through 1929. For some period around 1925, Beyer worked as a servant and governess for a family named Guinzburg in Westchester County (New York).

Beyer's life after 1927 and until her passing in 1944 is the period that can be reconstructed most clearly. During these years—specifically 1931 to 1943—she composed all of the music available today: works for piano, percussion ensemble, chamber groups, choir, band, and orchestra. During those years Beyer lived at three different New York addresses: 3961 Forty-Third Street (Long Island City, Queens); 40 Jane Street (Manhattan); and 303 West Eleventh Street (Manhattan). During 1934–35, Beyer had a scholarship for the New School for Social Research, and she taught piano for some time via the Federal Music Project. She studied composition briefly with Ruth Crawford, Charles Seeger, Henry Cowell, and possibly, in some capacity with Dane Rudhyar.[3] During Cowell's years in San Quentin Federal Penitentiary (1936–40), Beyer was extensively involved in his business affairs and in his family's campaign to gain early parole for him. In 1938 Beyer applied, unsuccessfully, for a Guggenheim fellowship; the curriculum vitae she created the year before remains today the sole source of information about certain details of her life and work.

Some evidence suggests that Beyer was diagnosed with multiple sclerosis in 1941, but according to her death certificate, she had been diagnosed with amyotrophic lateral sclerosis in 1938.[4] In early July 1943, shortly after writing her last dated piece, Beyer moved (or was moved) to an assisted-living facility in the Bronx called the House of the Holy Comforter, a free, Protestant, hospice-like home for women and child "incurables." She died there, six months later, on January 9, 1944. A funeral was held at the House of the Holy Comforter, and Beyer was buried in Kensico Cemetery, Westchester County, New York. Lou Gehrig is buried in the same cemetery, as is the Russian pianist Sergei Rachmaninoff and dozens of other notable figures. On the common gravestone erected for 104 women who died in the House of the Holy Comforter, the composer's name is misspelled—Johanna M. Bauer.

Beyer's fifty-six known compositions can be divided into several broad categories: piano music; percussion music; music with text; and mixed instrumental music. Her earliest known works are a waltz for piano (1931) and two solo clarinet suites (1932); her last dated works are a percussion ensemble piece called *Horizons* (April 1942) and the Sonatina in C for piano (June 1943). (See Appendices B and D herewith for a list of known compositions and currently available recordings.) Several undated works may have been completed in the year before her death. A number of scholars have insightfully analyzed much of Beyer's work, including Marguerite Boland, Ron Coulter, John Kennedy, Larry Polansky, and others. Conductor John McCaughey concluded, "Beyer's greatest talent is possibly as a melodist," and he made special note of her "dazzling textures, rhythmic overlays, sound-formations out of noise, and process forms."[5]

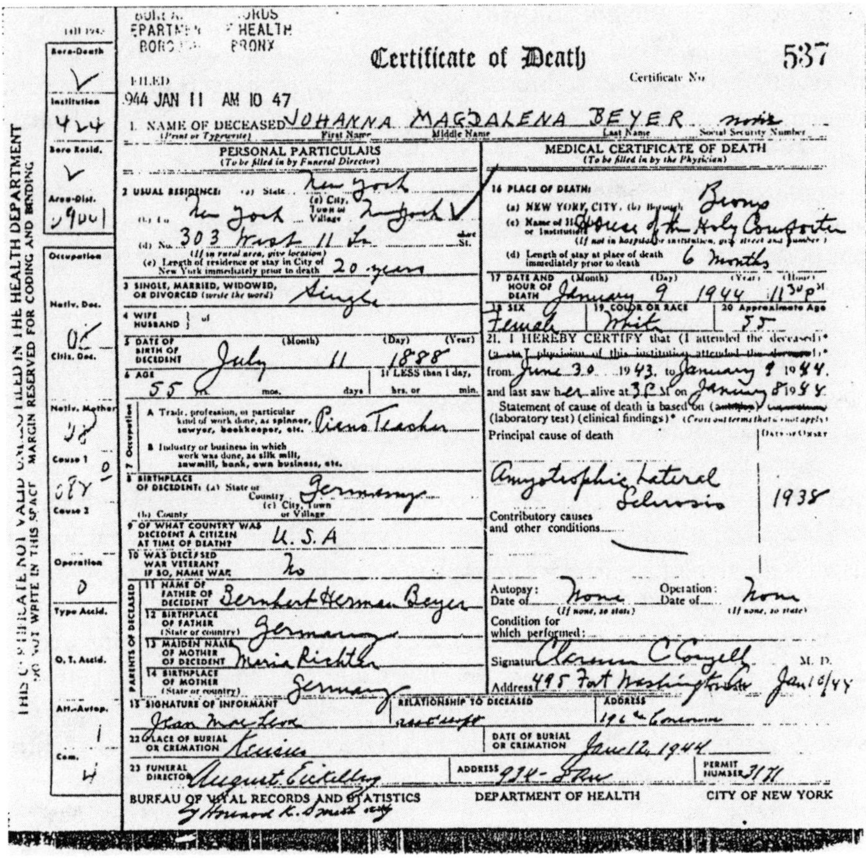

BUREAU OF RECORDS
DEPARTMENT OF HEALTH
BOROUGH OF BRONX

Certificate of Death 537

FILED 1944 JAN 11 AM 10 47

1. NAME OF DECEASED JOHANNA MAGDALENA BEYER

PERSONAL PARTICULARS (To be filled in by Funeral Director)

2. USUAL RESIDENCE: (a) State New York (b) Co. New York (c) City New York (d) No. 303 West 11 St.

(e) Length of residence or stay in City of New York immediately prior to death 20 years

3. SINGLE, MARRIED, WIDOWED, OR DIVORCED Single

5. DATE OF BIRTH OF DECEDENT July 11 1888

6. AGE 55

7. A Trade, profession, or particular kind of work done: Piano Teacher

8. BIRTHPLACE OF DECEDENT: State or Country Germany

9. OF WHAT COUNTRY WAS DECEDENT A CITIZEN AT TIME OF DEATH? U.S.A

10. WAS DECEASED WAR VETERAN? No

11. NAME OF FATHER OF DECEDENT Bernhart Herman Beyer

12. BIRTHPLACE OF FATHER Germany

13. MAIDEN NAME OF MOTHER OF DECEDENT Maria Richter

14. BIRTHPLACE OF MOTHER Germany

15. SIGNATURE OF INFORMANT Jean MacLeod — RELATIONSHIP TO DECEASED not kin

22. PLACE OF BURIAL OR CREMATION Kensico — DATE OF BURIAL OR CREMATION Jan 12 1944

23. FUNERAL DIRECTOR August Eickelberg

MEDICAL CERTIFICATE OF DEATH (To be filled in by the Physician)

16. PLACE OF DEATH: (a) NEW YORK CITY, (b) Borough Bronx (c) Name of Institution House of the Holy Comforter

(d) Length of stay at place of death 6 months

17. DATE AND HOUR OF DEATH January 9 1944 11:30 p.m.

18. SEX Female 19. COLOR OR RACE White 20. Approximate Age 55

21. I HEREBY CERTIFY that (I attended the deceased) from June 30 1943, to January 9 1944, and last saw her alive at 3 P.M. on January 8 1944.

Principal cause of death: Amyotrophic Lateral Sclerosis — 1938

Autopsy: None — Operation: None

Signature Clarence C. Coryell M.D. — Address 495 Fort Washington Ave. — Jan 10/44

BUREAU OF VITAL RECORDS AND STATISTICS — DEPARTMENT OF HEALTH — CITY OF NEW YORK

THIS CERTIFICATE NOT VALID UNLESS FILED IN THE HEALTH DEPARTMENT
DO NOT WRITE IN THIS SPACE — MARGIN RESERVED FOR CODING AND BINDING

Beyer's death certificate, filed January 11, 1944, Department of Health, Borough of the Bronx, New York.

Whatever renown Beyer has as a composer has endured primarily because of two achievements—one justified, and one misleading. The first—Beyer's pioneering contributions to the percussion ensemble repertoire—places her unquestionably among celebrated innovators in the medium—John Cage, Alejandro García Caturla, Lou Harrison, Amadeo Roldán, William Russell, and Edgard Varèse. The second reason Beyer's name is frequently evoked is because of characterizations of her composition *Music of the Spheres* (1938), scored "for three electrical instruments or strings." *Music of the Spheres* has repeatedly been discussed as the

House of the Holy Comforter gravestone, Kensico Cemetery, Walhalla, New York; Beyer's name (misspelled "Bauer") is in the third column, ninth from the bottom. Photograph by the author.

first work of "electronic music" written by a woman.[6] We do not know, in fact, what Beyer meant by "electrical instruments." She may have wished to have the work performed using the Theremin, a sliding-tone instrument she had occasion to observe when its inventor demonstrated its capabilities at the New School in February 1931, or perhaps an ondes martenot or other available "electrical" instruments of the time. The reputation of *Music of the Spheres*, no doubt enhanced by its evocative and celestial title, and the recording made in 1977 by the Electric Weasel Ensemble, has enchanted scholars and musicians with its mystery and has led many to make unconfirmed claims about historical firsts.

Though Beyer's music exemplifies the then-contemporary categories of dissonant counterpoint and ultramodernism, it is also deserving of a closer consideration on its own terms.[7] Her work combines the confidence of an original thinker and the calculations of an analytical mind. A fearless explorer in new methods of composition, including tempo melodies, serial techniques, clusters, sliding tones, and polyrhythm, Beyer designed innovative structures—often highly formalistic and economical processes—that demonstrate sensitivity to small details as well as larger designs. Lou Harrison recalled: "She had the typical 1920s and 30s attitude of geometry in music, or schemes that were carefully carried out and beautifully executed."[8] At the same time, Beyer's music is expressive, moving, and whimsical, and she occasionally used quotation for comic effect. Beyer allowed herself to move fluidly between abstraction and feeling, ultimately believing "that the heart and the brain should go hand in hand."[9] Chapters 4 through 8 of this book provide overviews of each broad category of composition, with particular pieces highlighted to demonstrate some of Beyer's greatest strengths as a composer.

Why is Johanna Beyer important? First, a growing number of scholars and musicians agree that she was an original composer in the school of American ultramodernism, whose compositions ought to be performed and analyzed alongside those of Henry Cowell, Ruth Crawford, and Carl Ruggles, and that her work—some fifty-six known compositions—deserves closer attention. Second, when one surveys her professional correspondence and the number of people who knew her as a pianist, composer, copyist, teacher, organizer, and advocate, it is baffling to realize how thoroughly she disappeared from the historical record. Judith Tick's exhaustive biography of Ruth Crawford Seeger (1997) mentions Beyer only once, though the women apparently knew each other well for a number of years. Michael Hicks, in his detailed account of Cowell's prison years (1991) and in his thorough biography *Henry Cowell, Bohemian* (2002), makes no reference to Beyer, though her eleven-year friendship with Cowell constituted one of her (and, arguably, his) most important relationships.[10] Leta Miller's 2006 article on the connections between Cowell and John Cage between 1933 and 1941 mentions Beyer only in passing, despite her importance as a pioneering composer of percussion ensemble music during exactly those years. Joel Sachs's recent biography of Cowell (2012) includes several brief mentions of Beyer, but only mentions once in passing that she was a composer in her own right.

Beyer research has gone through several stages since around 1970. Most important are Beyer's manuscripts themselves, almost all of which ended up at the American Music Center and are now in the Music Division at the New York Public Library.[11] The first efforts to assess her entire known body of work, most notably by John Kennedy and Larry Polansky in their article and catalog published in 1996, were based on her then-available manuscripts.[12] This collaborative project was inspired by Kennedy's initial work on Beyer with the ensemble Essential

Music. The second substantial source—some 115 letters Beyer wrote to Cowell, which are housed at the New York Public Library and were first made available to scholars in June 2000—provides details about Beyer's professional activities and her involvement in Cowell's personal and musical affairs between 1935 and 1941.[13] They paint a portrait of an intelligent, passionate, prolific, humorous, and troubled woman whose reading ranged from Friedrich Hölderlin's late-eighteenth-century epistolary novel *Hyperion* to Aldous Huxley's "Fashions in Love" (1929); from Richard B. Gregg's *The Power of Non-Violence* (1935) to Clarence Day's idiosyncratic view of humanity in *This Simian World* (1920). Her letters to Cowell mix dry professional arrangements with intimate, occasionally desperate love letters; further, they offer sometimes mundane, sometimes profound impressions of a piano teacher's exhausting commutes through Queens, Manhattan, Staten Island, and New Jersey, and allow us to witness her bravely suffering a degenerative illness.

A recently discovered source, surprisingly significant in its documentation of Beyer's life for seventeen years, is the diary of the pioneering educator and social worker Bertha Capen Reynolds (1885–1978).[14] Reynolds and Beyer met in 1927 and remained friends until Beyer's death. Reynolds's diary entries mention Beyer more than one hundred times. This diary, at long last, gives Beyer a rich identity, a context, and a circle of friends beyond Cowell, who has, perhaps unjustly, loomed too large, and for too long, in considerations of her biography.

Today, musicians who play Beyer's work are intrigued by her originality; theorists who study her methods are impressed by her formal ideas; and historians who search for new information about her are compelled by the dramatic arc of her life. In the reception gap that followed her death, she shares company with many great composers, from Johann Sebastian Bach to Scott Joplin, whose work also disappeared from a collective cultural consciousness for decades following their deaths. Leaps of deduction are frequently required of biographers lacking evidence due to clues missing or lost to history. In a review of a new 629-page book on Bach by John Eliot Gardiner, *New York Times* critic Zachary Woolfe writes: "Absent greater insights into Bach's life, scholars have tended toward romantic guesswork. Gardiner writes that the presence of what appear to be raindrops on a score owned by Bach indicates it 'may have traveled in his rucksack' during a youthful move from Ohrdruf to Lüneburg in 1700, but that's pure speculation."[15] In the following pages I have done my best to avoid "romantic guesswork" and "pure speculation," while trying to paint as vivid a portrait of Beyer as is possible at this time. The *American Composers* series is a fitting place for reassessing Beyer's life and work—some forty-five years after their rediscovery.

1 Sunnyside, 1927–1933

ASIDE FROM OFFICIAL PAPERWORK—birth and death certificates, residency registrations, ship manifests, passport numbers—the earliest currently knowable fact of Beyer's biography occurred in 1927, when she was thirty-eight years old. Therefore, our survey of Beyer's life begins on October 30, 1927, when the Smith College social worker Bertha Reynolds first recorded Beyer's existence in her diary. Now working at the Institute for Child Guidance and the Jewish Board of Guardians in New York, Reynolds sought a place to live outside the metropolis: "I had dreaded New York City as a home, feeling it would offer only the rock-bound canyons of a metropolis or exhausting commuting at the end of each day," Reynolds wrote later in her published memoir.[1] On a Saturday afternoon, she went to a new development in Queens called Sunnyside Gardens, at the suggestion of a co-worker. This housing project, begun in 1924, was still being built, and it featured two-story brick houses surrounding neighborhood green spaces meant for communal use. The housing development management office sent Reynolds to "a German music teacher, Miss Johanna Beyer," who had purchased one of the new homes and wanted to rent one of her rooms. Reynolds eloquently recorded this day, and the bucolic atmosphere in Beyer's neighborhood, in an "informal autobiography":

> I liked Miss B., engaged her east bedroom, and so started a friendship of 17 years, which ended with her death by multiple sclerosis. I shall never forget the satisfaction I felt in living close to the warm brown earth, hearing the rain fall on leaves, and seeing it soak into the ground in the garden under my window. I had been starved for the earth in city blocks and said that never again would I live that way. In twenty years I lived in Sunnyside I never lost my love for the green gardens and the whispering trees that grew there.[2]

In her published memoir, Reynolds wrote further of Sunnyside and Beyer: "I loved that Sunnyside community for all the twenty years it was my home, and my friendship with Miss Beyer lasted as long as she lived."[3]

Beyer's new house, in the southwest edge of the development near the crossing with Skillman Avenue, appears to have been registered as a new building with the New York City Department of Buildings in 1926. It is most likely that she became the first owner of this two-story structure in the section of Sunnyside called Madison Court in the summer of 1927; her name first appeared in the Queens directory in the winter of 1927–28.[4] The 1930 census lists the value of her home as $11,700.[5] The area was considered a special district for working-class housing, a planned seventy-seven-acre, garden-dominated community lined with sycamore trees, now managed as a National Register Historic District. By the mid-1920s the rapid transit system allowed residents to travel into the Forty-Second Street station in Manhattan in a mere fifteen minutes.

Clarence S. Stein, town planner and chief architect of Sunnyside Gardens, described the community feeling of activism in the housing project:

> There was one important difference between the people of Sunnyside and the others. Sunnyside was a community of people accustomed to meeting and doing things together—a real neighborhood community. The others were lone individuals with no organized social or other relations with the people who lived next door. At Sunnyside a home-owners' group was quickly formed; it comprised a majority of the community. The home-owners, as a community group, were soon ready to ask, and if necessary to fight, for a postponement of or a decrease in mortgage payments. In the end they went on strike and, as a group, refused to make payments.[6]

Sunnyside Gardens was the center of Beyer's social life.[7] Reynolds lived with Beyer for several years, and they were active with a circle of women friends and a number of Beyer's nieces. After a few years Reynolds moved to a different house in Sunnyside Gardens, a few blocks away from Beyer, at 3947 Forty-Eighth Street. The two properties were centers of activity for these women, and Beyer continued to spend time at Reynolds's house even after she moved to Manhattan in 1936. Friends in Beyer's community during this time included not just Reynolds and Beyer's niece Frida, who lived with Beyer for some period around 1930, but also the influential piano teacher Abby Whiteside, and Reynolds's cousin Erdix Winslow Capen (1909–1995), who was also a frequent visitor to the community.[8] After Reynolds moved out, Beyer rented briefly to Willard Espy (1910–1999), a writer for *World Tomorrow* who would go on to publish some twenty books, many of which were about wordplay, a practice in which Beyer apparently delighted. A later tenant of Beyer's named Elizabeth Rice was quickly integrated into Beyer's and Reynolds's circle of friends.

Reynolds's diary records details of Beyer's activities and dramatic events during the late 1920s. Shortly after Reynolds moved in, in November 1927, three of Beyer's nieces also occupied the household. A few months later, in March 1928, one of the nieces had a psychotic breakdown and disappeared; police found her days later and checked her into Kings Park Psychiatric Center in Brooklyn, where she died of heart failure within the week. In May 1928, another niece, Gertrude, visited and then married; a reception was held at Beyer's house (Gertrude and her husband would be among the few attendees at Beyer's memorial service in 1944). That summer, Reynolds paid Beyer twenty dollars to keep her room during her holiday travels; in July, Beyer and Frida took a vacation to Washington, D.C., where they were photographed in front of the Library of Congress.

Beyer's friendship with Reynolds seems to have brought her into a world of political activism and engagement with social and racial issues of the late 1920s and early 1930s. But Beyer had forged important friendships of her own before meeting Reynolds. In January 1928, Beyer met up with Reynolds at the International House (Morningside Heights), where Beyer introduced Reynolds to her friend, a young Trinidadian man named Francis Eugene Corbie (1891–1928), with whom the women then attended an art exhibit. It is presently unknown how Beyer first met Corbie, who was a well-known activist in public affairs and a prominent political speaker. City College's *Campus News* called him "the foremost undergraduate Negro student in America."[9] (Corbie also seems to have acted in a melodramatic comedy called *Cape Smoke; or, The Witch Doctor*, which ran at the Martin Beck Theatre in 1925.)[10] During the summer of 1928 Corbie became ill and returned to his family home in Port-of-Spain, Trinidad, where he died on October 3.[11] On a Sunday evening in November, Beyer and Reynolds attended Corbie's memorial service, held at the Community Church of New York and led by Rev. John Haynes Holmes, a pacifist known for his antiwar activism, and a cofounder of both the ACLU and the NAACP. A few years later Beyer would attend the NAACP annual meeting at St. Mark the Evangelist Church in Harlem.

Beyer's political engagement during this period embraced both national and international developments, and she and Reynolds were active in the Town Hall

Club, an important cultural and political center in Manhattan. In November 1928 Beyer and Reynolds attended a meeting about Franklin Roosevelt's New York gubernatorial campaign, and on New Year's Day 1929 Beyer gave a dinner party for a Mr. Arthur Moore and a woman involved in the Roosevelt campaign. Beyer also read avidly, keeping up on German politics with the help of the February 1929 issue of *Survey Graphic*, an issue devoted to "The New Germany 1919–1929," and she and Reynolds discussed the advantages of Germany's multiparty political system.[12] The women often spent time at a local coffeehouse and frequented several ethnic (Japanese, Indian) restaurants, no doubt eagerly discussing both local and global current events.

In January 1930 Beyer was naturalized as an American citizen; in July, with a new American passport in hand, she traveled to Germany for a two-month visit. On her 1930 passport application, she requested that her passport be mailed to an organization called Open Road Inc., which arranged for students and professional people to travel to Europe for the purposes of studying labor and socialist practices overseas, including in Soviet Russia. There is no indication that Beyer participated in one of these tours, but she may well have known the organizers of Open Road. This connection to a socialist-friendly group during this period of her life is not surprising, given all the evidence that places Beyer in the middle of a community of political activists sympathetic not only to socialist ideals and labor issues but also to racial and civil rights struggles.

On her 1930 passport application, Beyer listed her occupation as "music teacher." But Beyer's work during this period included both private piano teaching and professional accompanying in concerts, as well as work in dance studios.[13] For a time Beyer worked as an accompanist at the Denishawn School of Dancing and Related Arts, where Doris Humphrey taught dance until 1928. And as a conservatory-trained pianist, Beyer had the credentials to draw in paying piano students. She ran an advertisement for her piano studio in the November 1929 issue of the local *Sunnyside News*.

Beyer had at least one close competitor, a Sunnyside neighbor one block over named Helen Gollomb Tuvim (mother to actress Judy Holliday), who placed a similar ad in the September 1930 issue of *Sunnyside News*; Tuvim's "modern, progressive, psychological method" of piano teaching was going for a "special offer of $1.00 a lesson."[14] It is safe to assume that Beyer charged something similar.[15] Beyer also gave piano lessons to Reynolds, although it is unclear if money exchanged hands; together they studied, among other works, Schubert's "Unfinished" Symphony.

Amid all this social, political, and professional activity, Beyer's compositional

Advertisement for Beyer's private piano studio, published in *Sunnyside News*, November 1929; copy located by Herbert Reynolds in the E. E. Wood Papers, Avery Library Drawings and Archives, Columbia University.

imagination began to flourish, and it was in February 1931 that she composed and dated her earliest known work, a waltz for piano (now part of the *Cluster Suite*). Beyer's 1937 curriculum vitae also lists performances of original compositions from around this time, including a March 1931 performance of works Beyer composed for a dancer named Mara Mara at "An Exhibition of Persian Art and its Reaction on the Modern World," which opened with a special reception at the Brooklyn Museum. Her 1937 CV also lists among her accomplishments original music composed for dances at the innovative and experimental Dorsha Hayes Theater of the Dance. The worlds of socializing, politics, and culture were closely intermingled in the interwar years: on Memorial Day 1932, after hosting a birthday party for one of her friends, Beyer and her guests attended a Socialist Party meeting at P.S. 125 during which Dorsha and Paul Hayes entertained.

The spring of 1931 featured a number of musical events that may have helped lead Beyer down the path of ultramodernism and, eventually, to Henry Cowell: in February, Léon Theremin demonstrated his eponymous new instrument at the New School (Cowell would present his Rhythmicon there nearly a year later); that same month conductor Nicolas Slonimsky gave a Pan-American Association of Composers concert that included music by Cowell, Ives, Ruggles, Henry Brant, and Alejandro García Caturla; on March 31, Cowell gave a piano recital at the New School. In May 1931, the Greenwich Village Music Festival offered a program of compositions by Marion Bauer and other New York-based composers; Charles Seeger of the New School for Social Research spoke on Paul Hindemith's utilitarian concept of *Gebrauchsmusik* at the Greenwich House Music School.

As mentioned above, our earliest direct knowledge of Beyer's compositional work occurred in 1931; by January 1932 she was sharing her new work with her Sunnyside friends. Between February and May of that year, Reynolds documented three important facts—particularly significant for reviving Beyer's biography because her connection to the Seegers has long been discussed as a fact without any concrete evidence:

> 10 February: Johanna had interview w. Charles and Ruth Seeger—teachers of modern composition. They will give her lessons.
> 10 March: Johanna giving German lessons to Seegers to pay for comp. lesson every week.
> 12 May: Johanna composing.

That summer, Beyer submitted a piece to the arts competition at the Summer Olympics in Los Angeles.[16] In July and August she penned two poems—"Universal-Local" and "Total Eclipse"—which she would set to her own music two years later.

By the end of 1932 Beyer was having significant financial difficulties, and she hired workmen to refurbish her basement so she could live there while renting out the rest of her house; she had lost another tenant and was worried about her debts. Perhaps to distract her from such worries, Reynolds took her to a housewarming event for a socialist organization called Pioneer Youth of America; in January 1933 the friends attended a socialist meeting in Sunnyside "on Technocracy."

Beyer's friendships with Eugene Corbie, Bertha Reynolds, Dorsha Hayes, Abby Whiteside, Erdix Capen; her activities as an engaged aunt to many visiting nieces; her association with pacifists, socialists, left-wing sympathizers, and black activists during the Harlem Renaissance and the Depression; and her involvement in the Sunnyside Gardens community as a pioneering homeowner, landlady, music teacher, and hostess offer a much different view of her personality and social life than we have previously received, the latter a misleading history in which professional acquaintances described her as "strange and difficult to know," "angular, awkward, and self-conscious," "problematic," "extremely quiet," and, most condescendingly, "always there to lick stamps."[17] In fact, she led a rich life filled with accomplished people, intellectual pursuits, and compositional ambition. But our perspective on Beyer shifts dramatically around 1933. In this year of massive changes—Prohibition ended, Roosevelt took office, banks closed, Adolf Hitler was elected, and on and on—Beyer's musical and emotional world began to be dominated by her relationship with Henry Cowell and would remain so for much of the final eleven years of her life.

2 Compositional Beginnings, 1933–1936

BEYER'S COMPOSITIONAL BEGINNINGS soon brought her into the orbit of the New School for Social Research. For the 1933–34 school year, the New School listed among its instructors Henry Cowell, Roy Harris, Hanya Holm, Doris Humphrey, Harry A. Overstreet, Paul Rosenfeld, Charles Seeger, and Roger Sessions, among others. As the first fascism-fleeing wave of European immigrants started to descend upon New York, the New School became an important intellectual and cultural center. Sally Bick writes:

> Beginning in 1933, the School initiated advanced workshops in modern music that were addressed to a select group of students. These courses were directed toward students with professional aspirations in composition or were geared toward the adult student with higher intellectual goals. In both cases, the integrity of the materials would embrace the realm of pure learning. . . . The extraordinary musical activities initiated by Cowell and the community he fashioned launched the institution as an alternative platform in contemporary culture.[1]

Starting on September 27, 1933, Cowell taught a ninety-minute, ten-week Wednesday evening course called "Contemporary American Music," which included participation by a number of contemporary composers. Though Beyer does not appear on lists of registered students during the 1933–34 year, evidence suggests she visited this course, as well as Cowell's second course that fall, "Work

Course in Music: New Possibilities of Piano Playing."[2] Beyer's name first appears as a student in Cowell's fall 1934 class, "Creative Music Today," which included eleven students—all women except for Wallingford Riegger. Many years later Lou Harrison commented on Beyer's status as a student of Cowell's and, therefore, as part of an elite group of composers: "[She is] one of the siblings, therefore, of the hundreds of us who studied with Henry."[3]

We can only speculate about the specific occasion on which Beyer and Cowell first met. In early 1933, Reynolds's journal provides key information about Beyer's developing connections during this time:

> 9 March 1933: Johanna copying music for composer-teacher.
>
> 14 March 1933: Sunday night Johanna took us to a modern concert at the McDowell Club. Saw the Seegers and Ruth played song she wrote on poem re Sacco and Vanzetti by a Chinese Mr. Hysang [*sic*]. Henry Cowell played on piano strings like a harp.[4]
>
> 23 March 1933: Dinner with Johanna at Coffee House and then she played her comp.s. J. has chance to show her music to Henry Cowell for publication.

In addition to this evidence, Cowell's 1933 pocket calendar contains Beyer's name in several places. The first instance is on October 6, 1933, two days after the term's second class meeting of Cowell's course "Contemporary American Music": "12:30 Beyer," the entry reads. An article published in the *New York Times* on October 22 announced that "J. M. Beyer and Wallingford Riegger will discuss the relation of German to American music" on "Wednesday evening" (October 25) at the New School. On October 24, Cowell wrote: "4:00 rehearse Beyer." And on the day of the event in question, October 25, he wrote:

> Vanessa 5:00
> Class 5:30
> come early Beyer rehearse
> after Samaroff NS

According to her 1937 CV, Beyer's Three Songs for Soprano, Piano, and Percussion were performed at the New School on October 25, 1933. Aside from several solo pieces composed in 1931 and 1932—a piano waltz and two solo clarinet suites, respectively—Beyer composed several chamber pieces during 1933: a Percussion Suite in Three Movements; a Suite for Clarinet and Bassoon; a Quintet for Woodwinds; *Sky-Pieces* (a song setting of a poem by Carl Sandburg); and a set of three songs for soprano, piano, and percussion ("Timber Moon"; "Stars, Songs, Faces"; "Summer Grass"—also Sandburg). The last entry mentioning Beyer in Cowell's 1933 calendar is simply her Sunnyside address and phone number, at the back of the pocket notebook. Her contact information appeared on the same page as entries for Marion Bauer, Henry Brant, Aaron Copland, Wallingford Riegger, and Joseph Schillinger.

Beyer continued making strides in her compositional work and developed new working methods. In early 1934, exhausted from copying music by hand, she started using what Reynolds referred to as a "photo process for compositions"—most likely the ozalid printing process, first trademarked in the United States in 1929. Beyer also lost a job she had at this time playing for a dance instructor (probably at the Denishawn School mentioned in chapter 1). She also enjoyed a few performances of her own music: most notably, on February 15 the *Lentamente* movement from her Suite for Clarinet and Bassoon was performed at Cowell's New Music Society concert in San Francisco. (On February 20, 1934, Reynolds noted this in her diary: "One of Johanna's pieces played in the U. of Cal. New Music Soc.") A month later Reynolds wrote of "Johanna's concert in Boston," though it is unclear what this concert included, or where it took place. In late 1934 Beyer wrote a third poem, "To Be," which she set to music along with her 1932 poems "Universal-Local" and "Total Eclipse" in a collection titled Three Songs for Soprano and Clarinet. By December 1934, Reynolds noted that Beyer was gaining recognition for her music, but no money; she had also lost another Sunnyside tenant, leaving her without her small rental income.

Like most musicians during the Depression, Beyer struggled financially. Despite foreclosures and other threats, the year 1935 brought some relief through the Works Progress Administration and its associated initiatives, and it is probably during this time that she taught piano under the auspices of the Federal Music Project. Historian Richard Crawford writes of the significance of these programs:

> Between 1929 and 1934, about 70 percent of all musicians in the United States were unemployed, a trend the American Federation of Musicians, the national musicians' union, was powerless to buck. In 1935, as part of a massive relief effort labeled Federal Project Number One, under the Works Progress Administration (WPA), the national government took action, establishing the Federal Music Project as a way of supporting unemployed musicians. At its peak, the program employed 16,000 musicians, who gave 5,000 performances drawing an estimated monthly attendance of 3 million. . . . In addition, government funds were used to sponsor musicological research and to promote new music through the Composers' Forum-Laboratory. For the first time in the history of the United States, music was receiving systematic, comprehensive support.[5]

On the brink of the Federal Music Project era, we encounter the earliest currently available dated letter from Beyer to Cowell, written on February 12, 1935.[6] Writing from Sunnyside, she addressed him as Mr. Cowell and signed her name as it would appear on nearly all of her manuscripts: J. M. Beyer. The letter

Photograph included with Beyer's 1935 U.S. passport application. Photographer unknown; copy provided by United States Department of State, Passport Services, Department of Legal Affairs.

mostly describes a pedagogical method book she was composing at the time, a collection of short teaching pieces she called the "Piano-Book: Classic—Romantic—Modern" (to be discussed in chapter 4). The close of the letter adopted a flirtatious tone: "Do you want to join me for breakfast? Better hurry over before it gets cold."

For only the second (and last) time since her move to New York in 1923, Beyer traveled back to Europe from June until September 1935. Her passport application now listed her occupation as "music teacher and composer," as opposed to merely "music teacher" she had listed in 1930. In comparison with her 1930 passport photograph (reproduced on the cover of this book), the 1935 image reveals a visibly aged Beyer.

The immediate reasons for Beyer's trip were the occasion of her mother's eighty-fifth birthday and a performance by Beyer of "excerpts from different piano suites" at the twenty-fourth anniversary of the Society of Women Musicians in London on July13.[7] On or around that date, Beyer wrote a letter to Ruth Crawford and Charles Seeger on the back of a program she wanted Crawford to see.[8] This important letter not only verifies that Beyer did indeed travel to London in 1935 for a performance of her music but also reveals that she saw Adolf Hitler in person that summer—at the Leipzig Bach Festival:

> Dear Ruth, Charles, Michael, . . . and ?
>
> Have been thinking of you now and then and wonder whether you have grown in dimensions of family members, or whether it is still to be?
>
> I am stalking around in London since a week and have played at the 24th Anniversary of the Society for Women Musicians. Shall leave again for Germany the end of this week.

The Bach-Fest at Leipzig was great, quite interesting audience, one hears all kinds of languages, and saw also Hitler, crown prince, and princess—

Have to do a lot of traveling and visiting yet before I start back, which will be on Sept. 19th, the "Berlin."

I discovered your name on this program and thought you might be interested to see it. I had forgotten all about my birthday, till 2 days afterwards, but it was on July 11th, when I had tea with Miss K. Eggar, the Director of the Society. I told her then that to hear good American Music they ought to play your things before anybody else's, but she thought your percussion awfully peculiar! I must tell you more about it when I come to see you. I am on the latest program on English Members as just two American Guests. Hope so much all is well with you and here is my love

Hanna[9]

Shortly after Beyer's return to the United States, her Sunnyside house foreclosed. That fall, she composed a choral work called *The Robin in the Rain*, which she submitted to a Federal Music Project choral contest. At the same time, Beyer pursued her relationship with Cowell. Her second known letter to him, written on October 29, 1935, mentions neither details regarding her recent troubles (she was now living in her own basement, with nearly no heat) nor the fact that she was, at the moment, composing a five-movement percussion suite for nine instruments. (The fourth movement of this suite, *IV*, would be the only piece to be published during her lifetime, in Cowell's New Music Editions, 1936). Addressed "dear Henry," the letter included a romantic poem by Thomas Chalmers Robertson, which concluded with these lines:

For there each heart that beats is yours or mine,
and no voice can speak but it is ours,
till having each alone we shall not pine
for loss of the world, its prizes and powers.
Love, let me take our days into my arms,
and keep them close, to fend them from all harms.

"Do you like it?" she asked, before signing the letter, mysteriously, "Persephone."[10]

In early December, Reynolds once again chronicled Beyer's trials:

Johanna lives in basement and gets relief $1.00 a week for food. . . . May not get WPA job since she is "working." Homeowner's demonstration at Court House re foreclosures. The Seegers head up WPA in Washington and tell her no job for her.

Beyer's next letter to Cowell, written December 17, 1935, focused on her first impressions of his music:

I must start with the experience I had with your music from the very beginning. There was a time, when I went every week to the 58th [Street] music library to get modern music. It

> was there that I came upon one of your piano pieces. I had never seen written down anything of this kind and found it rather difficult to get [illegible], but by the end of the week I could manage a little and found out that there was someone who had the courage of writing down something similar to what I had come [?] sometimes, when improvising, or just wasting time on the piano. I just liked to listen to the sounds it made.
>
> When I heard you play the first time at the New School, I watched too much the mechanical part and I heard only 2 or 3 pieces. It was last year at the Irish Festival, when you played in the dim light, that it touched me for the first time, shortly afterwards you played again on the end of your course. I was just about to fall in the old habit of watching, when you said, it should not be watched. I obediently closed my eyes and felt for the first time to be able to shut out all prejudised [*sic*] conceptions of all times before, I felt that here was a music, which must be listened to differently and old terms could not be applied.

She further reflected on her reactions to a Town Hall concert in which Cowell played. She admitted that she was wondering what type of music she herself would write next, now that she had come so strongly under Cowell's influence: "You certainly have opened a wide field for me, you have taken the blindfold off my eyes and said: 'see, hear!' I am a lucky creature and certainly shall be grateful to you forever and ever. . . ." She closed her letter with the proclamation: "I dare to be your proud friend."

The year 1936 was a particularly fertile time for Beyer's growing body of work. On January 2, 1936, Reynolds noted that some of Beyer's works were to be played in Prague and Boston, and that she had sent music to a festival in Barcelona (no evidence has been located with regard to the Prague or Barcelona events). On January 22, Marion Bauer became the first woman to have a Composers' Forum-Laboratory concert; a few days earlier, Beyer had had an audition for a Composers' Forum concert of her own. During a brutally cold winter storm, Beyer traveled to Boston to hear clarinetist Rosario Mazzeo perform her Three Songs for Soprano and Clarinet on January 29.

The 1930s were a golden era for modern American music, and concert life, festivals, and competitions flourished. For example, in April 1936, *Musical America* announced: "Two prizes for orchestral compositions by native-born American composers will be awarded next season by the New York Philharmonic-Symphony Society and will be given performances by the orchestra."[11] The following month, *Musical America* announced a program of contemporary American music at the Music School Settlement, including work by Bauer, Beach, Copland, Cowell, Ives, and others. As an American citizen, but not a native-born one, and in the midst of rising immigration alongside Depression-era nationalism, Beyer's status may have hindered her success in taking advantage of certain performance opportunities for American composers, though she had been honored as one of "just two American Guests" at the London concert in July 1935. In a letter written several years later, Beyer expressed anger at Cowell for insisting she was not "100% American" and thus not eligible for certain festivals and competitions.[12]

Beyer had the first of her two Composers' Forum-Laboratory concerts on May 20, 1936, during which a number of her pieces were performed: Movement for Two Pianos (performed by Beyer and Jessie Baetz, also a student of Cowell's), "Excerpts from Piano Suites" (performed by Beyer); Suite for Soprano and Clarinet (performed by Rosario Mazzeo and Amelia Tartaronis); and her first string quartet (performed by the Modern Art Quartet). During the conversational "forum" with the audience after the performances, Beyer was asked about her favorite composer. She replied: "I don't think there is any favorite modern composer. I like Bach. I am influenced by Bach. Bach is my morning prayer and Bach is my evening prayer." When asked if she was influenced by Cowell or vice versa, she replied: "Well, I really don't know and probably Mr. Cowell doesn't know." Later she remarked: "I am not influenced by or imitating Henry Cowell at all." The transcription of the event records that when asked a pointed question about gender, Beyer "bowed graciously and the audience laughed."[13] Reynolds, who attended the event, was disappointed for her friend: "Johanna had her concert. They put her off till now, lost score, singers wouldn't sing and orch. wouldn't play till last minute. Played without heart. Questions insulting. But a few from good musicians, enthusiastic."

On May 21, one day after Beyer's Composers' Forum-Laboratory appearance and the same day the *New York Times* ran a short report about her concert, Cowell was arrested in Menlo Park, California, though Beyer would not learn of the event until he wrote to her a week later. [14] Due to alleged illegal sexual activity with underage boys, Cowell faced a "morals" charge. On July 8, 1936, after several weeks at the Redwood City Sheriff's office, he entered San Quentin Federal Penitentiary. While Cowell was in prison, from 1936 until 1940, Beyer served as the tireless caretaker of many of his professional affairs, and she corresponded extensively with many people, including his family, on his behalf. Though she looked after Cowell's business constantly during these years, she also composed close to thirty compositions in that same time, including *Have Faith!*—a short but powerful song for soprano and flute, begun several months after Cowell's arrest. The text, not coincidentally, expressed optimism about the future and revealed deep affection, if not love, as told in these lines:

But essential is, that you and I
and all the other things have faith
have faith in things to come
in things that passed, and are
and we must try to understand
and love and help each other.

3 Having Faith, 1936–1940

BEYER'S LIFE WENT THROUGH many changes in 1936, not the least of which was her move in September from her Sunnyside house and community—her home since 1927—to a small apartment at 40 Jane Street in the West Village.[1] Earlier that summer she started a new job teaching music in Harlem; perhaps this new steady income was the reason she could write to Olive Cowell (Cowell's stepmother) that she had "some money to spare."[2] Optimistically expecting Cowell to be released from his imprisonment soon, Beyer met frequently with the architect Alvin Johnson, director of the New School for Social Research at the time, and tried strategically to negotiate classes for Cowell to teach upon his return to freedom.[3] Much of Beyer's conversations with both Olive and Johnson focused on psychiatric appeals in Cowell's case, and on general views of homosexuality of the time.[4]

Beyer's health might have started to falter soon after Cowell's imprisonment; on one occasion she mentioned to Cowell that she had—or had had—cancer.[5] It is therefore all the more baffling that on August 31, 1936, she also wrote to Olive: "Fortunately I am healthy and can stand a lot of work." Beyer's second string quartet was completed the following month.[6] According to Beyer's death certificate, her ALS had its first onset a few years later, in 1938. In spite of her own personal battles during these years, between the summer of 1936, when

Cowell was jailed, and the summer of 1940, when he was released from prison, Beyer handled the majority of his business affairs, lobbied for his early parole, wrote dozens of letters, arranged performances, recordings, and radio airings of his work, and composed dozens of new works of her own.

Despite her move to Manhattan and her ongoing concern for Cowell's situation, she remained active in her Sunnyside circle of friends. On November 17, 1936, Reynolds's diary noted that Beyer attended a "theatre party," where Beyer, Reynolds, and Reynolds's cousin Erdix went to a benefit preview performance of Kurt Weill's *Johnny Johnson*, a satire on war that officially opened two nights later in a production directed by Lee Strasberg. After the show the friends had supper at an Indian restaurant in midtown called the Bengal Tiger, where the proprietor and his wife were musicians and dancers, and had friends in common with Beyer; Erdix bought recordings of Indian music from them.[7] A few days later, on November 20, 1936, Beyer claims (in the 1937 CV) to have had, at a place called the Central Manhattan Music Center, a Federal Music Project performance of a play she wrote called "The Modern Composer," for which she composed "incidental music, choreographed the modern ballet, designed and made the costumes, slides, illustrated advertisements, directed the whole play, [and] took the piano part." Given the specificity of these details, it is difficult to doubt the veracity of her claim; yet neither evidence of the performance nor her writings or music for this piece have surfaced.[8] Around this time Beyer and Reynolds also attended a Theatre Union play called *Marching Song*, written by John Howard Lawson, who had once served as the leader of the Hollywood branch of the Communist Party USA.

During this period Beyer's life seemed to balance precariously between a private struggle with poverty and being on the brink of public recognition. Beyer received some support from WPA projects around this time, but Reynolds noted that she "keeps warm with gas radiator lugged from room to room." In April 1937, Beyer attended a Sunday afternoon reception for Paul Hindemith at the Greenwich House Music School. A group photograph of the participants at the event—nearly fifty people, only a handful of whom are identified—appeared on page 33 of the May 10, 1937, issue of *Musical America*.[9] At the event Beyer met Irma Goebel Labastille and Marion Bauer, with whom she discussed Cowell's case and the need for sending letters to the prison board.[10] During this time Beyer also tried to find a publisher for Cowell's book manuscript "The Nature of Melody," contacting publishers Knopf, Fischer, and Schirmer, and enlisting the help of Aaron Copland, Otto Luening, Nicolas Slonimsky, and others.[11]

WORKS PROGRESS ADMINISTRATION
Federal Music Project
of New York City

COMPOSERS' FORUM-LABORATORY
Second Series Nos. 38 & 39
Directed by Ashley Pettis

Wednesday Evening, May 19th, 1937 - 8:45 o'clock

WPA FEDERAL MUSIC THEATRE
254 West 54th Street
New York City

COMPOSERS - JOHANNA M. BEYER and WALTER HELFER

P R O G R A M

JOHANNA M. BEYER

I. SONATA FOR CLARINET AND PIANO (1936)
(Dedicated to Rosario Mazzeo and Nicolas Slonimsky)

William Bortman, clarinet
Composer at the piano

II. SUITE FOR CLARINET AND BASSOON (1933)
Allegro ritmico quasi presto
Lentamente
Allegro grazioso
Allegro ponderoso

William Bortman, clarinet
Herbert Coleman, bassoon

III. EXCERPTS FROM PIANO SUITES (1930-1936)

Composer at the piano

IV. SUITE FOR VIOLIN AND PIANO (1937)
(Dedicated to Szigeti and Magaloff)

Carmela Ippolito, violin
Composer at the piano

V. QUINTET FOR WOODWINDS (1933)
In one movement

George Lisitzky, flute
Samuel Spumberg, oboe
William Bortman, clarinet
Ralph Capocci, English horn
Herbert Coleman, bassoon

Composers' Forum-Laboratory program for Beyer's second concert, May 19, 1937; copy located by Melissa J. de Graaf in the National Archives and Records Administration, College Park, Maryland.

On May 19, 1937, Beyer had her second Composers' Forum-Laboratory event, shared with composer Walter Helfer.[12] The printed program for this concert included what has been thought, until just recently, to be the only photograph of Beyer in existence (the passport photos included on the cover of this book and in chapter 1 are the only other known photographs of Beyer).[13] Beyer again performed "Excerpts from Piano Suites (1930–1936)"; the Suite for Violin and Piano (performed by Carmela Ippolito, violin, and Beyer); Sonata for Clarinet and Piano (1936; dedicated to Rosario Mazzeo and Nicolas Slonimsky; performed by William Bortman, clarinet, and Beyer); Suite for Clarinet and Bassoon (1933; Bortman, clarinet, and Herbert Coleman, bassoon). Her Quintet for Woodwinds appeared on the program but was not performed for lack of time. During the conversation with the audience after the concert, in response to a question about scales versus clusters, Beyer remarked: "I think that this modern life is so noisy, so intricate, and so complicated that one just can't explain it any more with one simple tone and melody. One must simply go on and bang like the rest of the world." Another audience member asked: "Was Miss Beyer ever in love?" She responded cryptically: "I have never been out of it." Beyer was also questioned about the difference between composing from one's head as opposed to one's heart. Here she might have been reminded of what Charles Seeger wrote about Ruth Crawford in *American Composers on American Music* (1933) with regard to the difference between "reason" and "aesthetic effect": "Serious music must be capable of submission to both tests. It is a co-operation of head and heart, of feeling and thinking. The trouble with so much modern music is that there is a fight on between the two—the head is afraid to think and the heart cannot feel, or vice versa. Composers, take notice!"[14]

In August 1937, Cowell was sentenced to fifteen years in prison, with parole denied and "no further parole consideration until one-half of the sentence is served."[15] Olive informed Beyer of Cowell's sentence that same month, while Beyer was spending the summer at Reynolds's house in Sunnyside.[16] Olive enlisted Beyer in a cause that, in fact, already occupied her and would for the next three years: "With much appreciation for all your efforts and as soon as plans are matured, I shall let you know what you can do in New York."[17] When Beyer received Olive's letter, she already knew of the sentencing. Ten days prior, Cowell himself had written, reassuring Beyer that he was trying to maintain a positive attitude and to continue working. At the time, Beyer was writing her first orchestral composition—on August 5, 1937, Reynolds noted, "Johanna writing a symphony"—and on August 8 Beyer herself wrote to Koussevitzky: "I have just finished my First Symphony." Cowell encouraged her to continue copying parts (Koussevitzky had, at least, agreed to look at the work) and expressed his enthusiasm over the possibility that the conductor might eventually perform the piece. Regarding their personal relationship, he wrote, "You have been wonderful in writing so often, and I enjoy every letter from you greatly. If you wish to continue writing them, I shall be delighted. But if you find, that it is upsetting to you, to continue, I shall understand this perfectly. Sometimes I feel, that part of you is being imprisoned, because of the closeness of the contact in letters, and perhaps you would be setting yourself free by breaking off the contact."[18]

To the contrary, Beyer's devotion seems to have deepened as she took on more and more administrative responsibilities for Cowell. Her feelings for him were also revealed in a number of suggestive letters to Olive. On August 30, 1937, Beyer wrote Olive a particularly emotional—and unconfirmed—account of a seduction, refusal, and possible engagement with Cowell. That fall, Beyer also composed an orchestral work titled *CYRNAB*—an unusual but revealing conflation of hen**RY**Cowell and johan**NAB**eyer.[19]

In some ways Beyer seems like two different women during this period. She was emotionally overwrought about Cowell's situation and overwhelmed by her increasingly romantic feelings for him. At the same time, she composed prolifically—in 1937 alone she wrote eight works, including two chamber pieces, three pieces for choir, and three works for orchestra—while copying her own and Cowell's music, conducting a variety of business tasks for him, and continuing her teaching obligations.[20] She participated in a meeting for the founding of the American Composers Alliance (ACA) in December 1937, alongside Marion Bauer, Marc Blitzstein, Paul Bowles, Otto Luening, Wallingford Riegger, Virgil Thomson, and Edgard Varèse.[21] Beyer corresponded frequently with Olive about various financial issues pertaining to her promotion of Cowell's music—getting scores copied and bound, paying his ACA dues, and so on. Toward these ends, Olive kept money in an account of Cowell's that Beyer could access. In September 1939, Beyer told Olive, "This is one of the most busiest months." She added:

> I am writing to all the conductors I can think of, send scores and get parts ready and so on. Had a fine letter from Stokowsky [*sic*], he wants Henry's scores in Philadelphia in October and Nicolas Slonimsky just called up, he spoke of the possibility of having Henry recorded with the Columbia Phonograph Co. I have to get in touch with them Monday and see what I can do to help it along. And so on . . . [22]

In addition to the activities recorded in Beyer's letters to Cowell and to Olive (and others), Cowell's own San Quentin–era letters to Olive reveal to what degree Beyer had taken charge: he reported to Olive that Beyer wrote to him frequently about radio broadcasts of his work, that she communicated with Blanche Walton regarding the copying of scores and parts for orchestral engagements, negotiated fees for performances and recordings, and undertook meetings and communications on his behalf (and sometimes her own) with Leopold Stokowski, Nicolas Slonimsky, Percy Grainger, Walter Fischer, Harrison Kerr, Gerald Strang, Martha Graham, Fabien Sevitzky, Hans Kindler, Joseph Schillinger, Ashley Pettis, Lazare Saminsky, Dorothy Lawton, Alvin Johnson, Edwin A. Fleisher, Arthur Cohn, Joseph Szigeti, Harry Allen Overstreet, the Leunings, the Seegers, Aaron Copland, Alfred Wallenstein, Howard Barlow, the Columbia Phonograph Company, the Columbia Broadcasting System, and many others.[23] She was fearless in her reaching out for help for Cowell's work.

Around 1938 Beyer was included in a small group that would comprise a "Promotion Committee" for the New Music Quarterly Recordings (NMQR), and she communicated regularly about the New Music recordings project with Harrison Kerr, Otto Luening, and Gerald Strang, who had taken over the direction of New Music Society events. At this time Beyer also provided to Luening (who, from his office at Bennington College, served as a chairman to the executive committee overseeing NMQR while Cowell was in prison) a particularly personal mailing list for possible future member subscribers to the NMQR project, a list that included Rosario Mazzeo, Erdix Winslow Capen, the Overstreets, Sunnyside resident Professor Otto Koischwitz, Martha Graham company member Nina Fonaroff, the Guinzburgs (Beyer's employers in 1925, now living on Park Avenue), and Beyer's fifteen-year-old piano student in Harrington Park, New Jersey, named "Rudi" (Rudolph Radama von Abele, who would go on to earn a doctorate in American history at Columbia University).[24] Beyer also connected Luening to Percy Grainger, who agreed to have his name listed as a "Patron" for NMQR. Though Cowell took pains to avoid further emotional commitment with Beyer, he clearly recognized her devotion to promoting his work.[25] In February 1938, he responded to Walton's evidently negative opinion of Beyer, significantly referring to her as a "friend" rather than as a former student or "secretary":

> I am sorry that [Beyer] did not make a favorable impression on you. She has done such a lot for me—has gone to endless pains, taken endless time, made so many calls on my behalf, that I am greatly endebted [*sic*] to her. She was not one of my best acquaintances; yet she is the only one in NY who remains there steadily who seemed to be willing and offered to do all these things. . . . It would seem that among my friends she is the only one who was in a position to do it, and also wished to. And I am very grateful indeed to her. Her faithfulness and tirelessness have been a matter of wonder to me. I do wish that she was just the right person in your estimation![26]

Perhaps as a way of publicly thanking Beyer, in 1938 Cowell composed a three-movement solo piano piece called *Rhythmicana*, which he dedicated to her.

When Cowell thought Beyer was coming west on tour with "a Chinese dancer" named C. Chew in 1939, he wrote to his father: "I hope you can show her a bit of hospitality while she is here. . . . She has done more errands for me, and ungrateful tasks such as copying orchestra parts, than anyone else, almost at least in the east."[27] In 1940, Cowell again acknowledged his gratitude, writing to his friend John Becker: "I have had a flurry of performances lately—Johanna Beyer's efforts for my music have borne fruit."[28] At the same time, Beyer worked to make practical arrangements for Cowell's parents, who planned to visit New York City in mid-March. For the occasion of their visit, she arranged a concert at the Downtown Music School and created advertising for the event herself.[29]

Beyer was also indefatigable as a pianist in promoting Cowell's newest work. She recorded his *Tocanta* for Hanya Holm, who wanted to use the work in a dance. Beyer sent Olive the bill with the announcement, "I have to meet Fabien Sevitzky tomorrow on account of the March 28th performance over the radio."[30] On February 11, 1940, several months before his release, Beyer performed *Rhythmicana* and *Tocanta* at an all-Cowell Composers' Forum-Laboratory concert. Later that month, Beyer listened to a radio performance of Cowell's *Old American Country Set* by Sevitzky and the Indianapolis Symphony—a performance for which she was personally responsible. She wrote to the conductor—Koussevitzky's nephew and one-time principle bassist for Stokowski, who became the conductor of the Indianapolis orchestra in 1937—in a manner symptomatic of her fervent reaction to music:

> I had hoped to be able to stay here and listen in quietly to be closer to composer-music-conductor, but it so happened that I had to share it with friends in a different place. Three of us were sitting on a sofa, the *Old American Set* score on my lap. I am used to be alone, other people disturb me in listening as I like to, yet, the moment the music started, I felt your great personality. I seemed to see and feel every one of your moves. You conduct with heart and soul and I hardly think anyone could ever go to sleep while you conduct, there is always that striking vitality, stirring. And I felt Henry and was deeply touched by his delightful, sweet, lovely dance-music—my heart ached that it had to be over so quickly, I could have listened on and on. It is wonderful to know you![31]

Sevitzky responded kindly on March 9, 1940. In what appears to be the last recorded attempt of Beyer to promote her own work, she wrote to Sevitzky a few months later, asking if he would look at some of her compositions, namely, what she called Symphonic Movement I (1939) and Symphonic Opus 5 (1940). She informed him, "The Symphonic Movement was selected by Dr. Hans Kindler,

Washington, among the best incoming works, so was one of Henry Cowell's, however we both did not get played there after all!"[32] Though Sevitzky and Beyer met and talked at length when he was in New York City in late spring 1940, the conductor never programmed any of her orchestral compositions.

On April 9, 1940, a federal census taker recorded the residential details of Beyer's apartment building at 40 Jane Street. Rather than "Johanna Beyer," an "Elsie Beyer" is listed as a resident of the building. The census-documented age of this woman was thirty-nine years old (Johanna Beyer would have been fifty-one at the time), and the report says she was born in New York. "Elsie," the sole resident of the apartment, gave her occupation as music teacher. The census says she has no education beyond high school. Her salary is listed as $1,000 for fifty hours' work in 1939. I have found no other reference to an "Elsie" in any Beyer-related documents. It is unclear whether Beyer deliberately lied to the census taker about her name, age, place of birth, and level of education, or if something else occurred to obscure the facts. Existing evidence, in particular the large volume of correspondence Beyer wrote during the spring of 1940, strongly suggest she was living at 40 Jane Street at the time. Why these inaccuracies were recorded in the 1940 census presently remains a mystery.

Before Cowell's sentencing was reconsidered in April 1940, Beyer again solicited letters of support from the contemporary music world at large. She asked them to write letters on official letterhead paper to the Board of Prison Terms and Paroles, San Quentin, and requested that the letters be sent directly to her so she could deliver them collectively to the prison, "so that they may be at hand at the psychological moment."[33] On March 24 she wrote, exasperatedly, to Grainger: "The case is postponed to the first week in May and I am supposed to send off all the letters directly to the Board on April 25th. If I had the time and strength I would copy these many letters, for they all came open, except the one from Ives; alas, I might as well give up."[34] A few weeks later, in a hastily hand-scribbled note, she told Sevitzky, "Henry Cowell is coming back in a short time!—we have been successful at last!"[35]

As Cowell began to prepare for his life after his June 1940 release from prison and his move to Grainger's house in White Plains, New York (where, as a condition of his parole, he would work as Grainger's "secretary"), Beyer was among a very small group of people besides Grainger and Cowell's parents—"a few very trusted friends"—who were kept informed of his whereabouts.[36] Cowell explained further to Grainger: "I have also asked Hanna to aid in preventing you from being pestered in any way, and in protecting against any publicity. Unfortunately she is not very strong now, but she is quite willing to act as a buffer in receiving letters and calls, etc., instead of their going to White Plains."[37] This letter contains one of Cowell's few known acknowledgements of Beyer's declining health, a factor he seems to have ignored after he began to disengage from her friendship and her professional support.

4 New York Waltzes

Works for Piano

BEYER WAS A SKILLED PIANIST, so it is not surprising that she wrote a number of solo piano pieces. The titles for her three major piano suites (*Gebrauchs-Musik*; *Dissonant Counterpoint*; and *Clusters*) derive from techniques in the air during the mid-1930s. Beyer's use of the term *Gebrauchsmusik* (or, as she wrote it, "*Gebrauchs-Musik*") must have been ironic, given the atonal and abstract nature of her pieces under that title. Beyer may have become aware of the principles of Gebrauchsmusik—a German term for "utilitarian music," or music that served some specific social or situational function—through a lecture given by Charles Seeger on Paul Hindemith's use of the concept, in May 1931 at a New School–sponsored festival held at the Greenwich House Music School.[1] In her 1933 book on modern music, composer Marion Bauer summarized Gebrauchsmusik: "It deals with the 'sociological function of music,' and has as a basic idea that music—good or bad—is futile if it cannot attract an audience."[2]

Beyer's *Gebrauchs-Musik* consists of five short, mostly two-voice pieces. The undated *Dissonant Counterpoint* likewise explores repeating and evolving rhythmic patterns, as well as additive rhythm ideas, expanding the length of individual measures within an ametrical setting—not unlike Olivier Messiaen's technique of additive rhythms—and creating discretely separate phrase structures similar to techniques used in her clarinet suites. Like much of Beyer's music, these pieces frequently include difficult polyrhythms (three against four; four against five; five against six). The fourth movement of *Dissonant Counterpoint* features a serial treatment of intervals in each of the two voices. This all-interval set of outwardly expanding mirror construction is analogous to similar precompositional designs used by Béla Bartók (*Music for Strings, Percussion, and Celeste*, 1936) and Anton von Webern (Piano Variations, op. 27, also 1936). Beyer frequently used octave displacement to obscure intervallic unity (*Gebrauchs-Musik* IV).

Several pieces suggest Beyer was thinking in terms of twelve-tone constructions. In *Dissonant Counterpoint* IV and VIII, Beyer's use of a slow, quiet, sparse texture, with frequent interruptions by silence, foreshadow what would later come to be known colloquially as "Feldmanesque." Further restrictions of material often include choice of pitch and limitations of range. The pieces in these suites tend to alternate between a quick, rhythmic style and a slow, static one. Like most of Beyer's other piano works, these suites were intended for the composer to perform herself. The manuscript source for *Dissonant Counterpoint* includes penciled-in phrases in Beyer's hand with mood indications like "Problems" (III), "Happy-go-lucky" (V), and "Religion" (VI).

Because of the many gaps in Beyer's biography, we are left without a clear impression of how she might have "stumbled into herself" as a composer, to borrow a description of Ruth Crawford's compositional self-awakening—although Beyer's mentioning to Cowell of "improvising, just wasting time at the piano" suggests how her stumbling might have begun.[3] Her earliest known work, the waltz dated 1931, is a seventy-two-bar solo piano piece, the first in a set of four short pieces she would eventually call *The Cluster Suite*. (Bertha Reynolds first mentions Beyer's own works in a diary entry on January 8, 1932, a little over a month before she had her initial "interview" with the Seegers.) Beyer performed this piece (or sections of it) on May 20, 1936, as part of "excerpts from piano suites, 1930–35" in her Composers' Forum-Laboratory event. In her program notes for the concert, Beyer described another piece in a gendered manner: "Two-part dissonant counterpoint; the first voice feminine, arabesque-like; the second voice strong, masculine." She might have been referring to the first piece of *Dissonant Counterpoint*, with its smoothly legato, slowly moving left hand, and its bouncy, rhythmically nervous right hand.

Beyer's "excerpts from piano suites" seem to have been a combination of *Dissonant Counterpoint* and a set of four pieces she grouped as *The Cluster Suite*. Beyer's program notes for the event refer directly to her earliest piece, written in 1931, which she "satirically" called a "waltz": "Doris Humphrey called it once 'architectural.' After an introduction of nine measures the theme enters and stays

Dissonant Counterpoint IV, piano; manuscript held in the Music Division, New York Public Library for the Performing Arts.

on the scene almost unchanged, only its environment changes. It was danced by Dorsha [Hayes] in 1930–31." On May 19, 1937, Beyer again played "excerpts from piano suites" in her second Composers' Forum-Laboratory concert. Her program notes for that performance also referred to the "Original New York Waltz," which eventually became the third piece in *The Cluster Suite*:

> A group of chords is gradually interpolated, finally running off in dissonant contrapuntal passages only to be summoned again. Organized rests, rests within the measure, whole measure rests, 1, 2, 3 measure rests, tonally and rhythmically undergo all kinds of crab forms. Throughout, the tone "F" is reiterated. Around it, tones are grouped singly, becoming more substantial; chord clusters part again, to stay on singly but one or two groups of tone clusters get acquainted with a single melody. A struggle for dominance between group and individual seems to overpower the latter; yet there is an amiable ending.

During the question-and-answer period after the concert, an audience member asked: "Please identify the numbers from the Piano Suite which you played. The third movement was strange and remarkably moving." Beyer simply responded: "I have no names to my music. I have just numbers." Despite this refusal to admit to programmatic intentions, Beyer was clearly thinking in dichotomous terms at least some of the time—masculine/feminine; group/individual, and so on.

The Cluster Suite exhibits traits typical of dissonant counterpoint. These pieces also reveal Beyer's ability to write strong melodies, rhythmically driving motives, and nonthematic material that exploits the power and range of her instrument. Two of the pieces in the suite are set in triple meter (the above-mentioned 1931 waltz and "the original New York waltz"), and these two are also most suggestive of tonality. The "original New York waltz" is almost entirely monophonic and *pianissimo*; the piece that precedes it features five- and six-octave clusters played *fortissimo*. The four short pieces are connected by a five-bar "starting motive," which was meant to be played at the beginning, then between each piece, and at the end, giving the suite a sense of formal coherence. This "starting motive" consists entirely of two-octave-wide forearm clusters. Throughout the four pieces, Beyer makes extensive use of fist, wrist, and forearm clusters. Though the manuscript of *The Cluster Suite* bears no named dedicatee, it strongly suggests an homage to one of the main promoters of the cluster technique, the same man who "opened a wide field" for Beyer's music: Henry Cowell.[4]

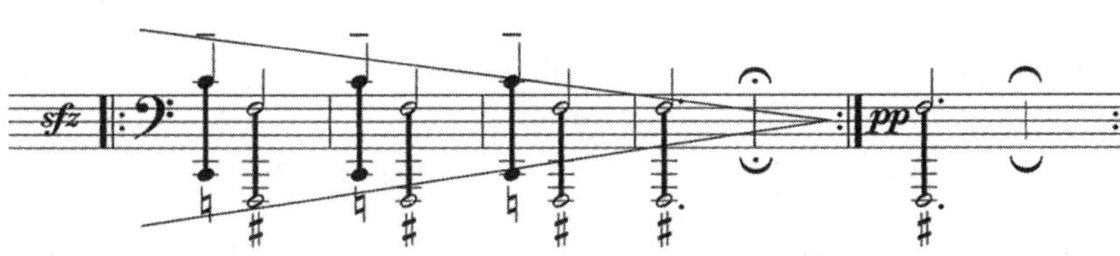

"Cluster" motive, from *The Cluster Suite*, piano; edited by the author with Dennis Bathory-Kitsz and Larry Polansky. Used by permission of Frog Peak Music.

Several of Beyer's later piano pieces return to a more tonal idiom, though these shorter works seem to have been written more for private consumption or for teaching purposes than for the concert hall. These include the three-movement Suite for Piano (1939), dedicated to Henry Cowell; an undated, thematically simple Prelude and Fugue in C Major; and a Sonatina in C—dated "Greenwich Village, N.Y., June 1943" and dedicated to Beyer's piano student Roland Leitner. Her formal choices—suite, sonatina, prelude, and fugue—might also reflect the cultural move toward neoclassicism at the expense of modernist experimentation during the Depression years. In an undated letter to Cowell written around 1940, Beyer talked of her piano students' involvement with the Suite for Piano, which several of them were playing: "Rudi had asked me to give him a copy of my latest piano suite, he heard Roland play it and likes it very much. Now he hums the themes!"

Beyer's last known piece, the Sonatina in C, is in four short movements (Allegro brioso; Scherzo-Trio; Andante; and Sciolto). The pieces contain exclusively Italian markings, including some rather uncommon terms, such as "scorrendo," "tardando," "tenero," "tempo frettoloso," "misterioso ma con rigore," "cantalerle," and "ridotto," among others. The pieces are charming and beautiful, and they contain many of Beyer's favorite ingredients (dance-like melodies, clusters, extreme registers, polyrhythm, 5/4 meter, rondo-like developments of main themes). The Sonatina raises several troubling questions, however, given that it is dated June 1943, just six months before her death. (Beyer moved to the House of the Holy Comforter on [or around] July 4, 1943, according to Bertha Reynolds's diary.) It is hard to imagine Beyer writing this piece so clearly, given that within six months she would be dead from an illness that normally deprives its victims the use of their hands at some point. Indeed, the title, name, and date on the first page appear to be printed in someone else's hand. The dedication to Beyer's beloved piano student Roland Leitner also raises questions. Was he still taking piano lessons from her at this late date? Did he visit her in her West Eleventh Street apartment in Greenwich Village and help her with her daily needs, including titling and dating a work perhaps written years earlier?

The undated short composition called *Bees* demonstrates the composer's poetic nature and her delight in programmatic references. With the tempo marking "As fast as possible (The bees are busy)," the piece zips along in a series of chromatic trills and scales, imitating the buzz of a moving bee. (The piece is similar in many ways to Béla Bartók's "Buzzing," which appears as #63 in Book II of *Mikrokosmos*, composed between 1926 and 1939.) Beyer's *Bees* exists in several versions, one of which contains lyrics about happy bees gathering honey from flowers and

Sonatina in C (1943), excerpt, piano; manuscript held in the Music Division, New York Public Library for the Performing Arts.

trees. The words were "probably intended pedagogically," for singing or recitation, with the sounds "sr—" and "br—" accompanying the tremolos and trills.[5]

The larger collection in which one version of *Bees* appears, called by Beyer *Piano-Book* with the subtitle "classic—romantic—modern," contains a number of original pedagogical pieces as well as arrangements of several folksongs (like the German tune "Winter Ade," the Christmas carol "Stille Nacht" ["Silent Night"], a French folk song, and others).[6] The book also includes doodle-like line drawings of plants, people on a see-saw (one of the pieces is called *See Saw*), stick figures standing on hills, and something that looks like a sea otter. Beyer wrote lyrical poetry for nearly every piece in the *Piano-Book*. Much like Bartók's *Mikrokosmos*, Beyer's *Piano-Book* trusts the beginning piano student to quickly grasp concepts like cross rhythms, improvisation, echo games, contrary/mirror motion, transposition, "difficult" keys, rolled chords, chromatic scales, hand crossings, syncopation, and other techniques infrequently found in traditional method books for young pianists.

In a 1935 letter to Cowell, Beyer described the *Piano-Book* in this way:

> The outward form is grouped in Four Seasons: Winter, Spring, Summer, Fall. I started with winter, yes. Each little piece has a rhyme and a picture. . . . All the years of teaching and never finding the right books and looking over the dozens of books at Schirmers (I must confess I only looked at them for a few minutes) with their few good things here and there, but never together, have helped. I have used all idioms I know exist and are possible: classicism, romanticism, modernism. There are also suggestions and appliance for transposition. In echo games I have urged creating musical answers, leading towards composition.

One version of "Winter Ade" ("Goodbye Winter") was stamped by the American Music Center on August 5, 1936, and is labeled "German Folksong with various versions." The set as it is currently archived includes pieces labeled "Italian Folksong," "Russian Folksong," "Ireland," "England—old popular song 1672," and "Switzerland—1839." It is unclear for what these pieces were intended; Kennedy and Polansky note that several of these works were not variations on "Winter Ade" but rather nation-specific tunes like "Volga Boatman" and "Santa Lucia."[7]

In addition to her solo and pedagogical pieces for piano, Beyer composed one piece she called simply Movement for Two Pianos, also aptly dedicated to Cowell. The piece focuses on polyrhythm (the main theme is seven against three), rolled clusters, clusters played as increasingly loud tremolos, multi-octave clusters played fortissimo, and other sonic shock effects. Beyer provided the following notes for her performance of this piece with Jessie Baetz at the 1936 Composers' Forum-Laboratory concert:

> Written in 1936 for the composer-pianist-painter Mrs. Jessie Baetz and dedicated to Henry Cowell, because it brings in its development tone-clusters, which he originated, as you all know. Each piano part has its own independent, individual theme, even themes, yet together they strive to make a whole and succeed, just because of their individual independence. One stresses more the tonal element, the other the rhythmic.

Like much of Beyer's music, the Movement for Two Pianos is dramatic, effective, and thematically unified.

In a rare, candid moment of graciousness, Henry Cowell once wrote: "I remember Beyer's playing as having the composer's intelligence behind it."[8] As a pianist, teacher, and composer, Beyer made the piano central to all her musical experiences. Her compositions for piano constitute a substantial and innovative body of work for this instrument.

5 Horizons

Percussion Ensemble Music

BETWEEN 1933 AND 1942, Johanna Beyer composed eight works for percussion ensemble—a total of nineteen movements and about seventy-five minutes' worth of music. Copies of five of these pieces were archived in the Edwin A. Fleisher Collection of Orchestral Music in the Free Library of Philadelphia. Frank J. Oteri has called Beyer "after William Russell, . . . the single most prolific composer of percussion music in the 1930s."[1] Beyer's four suites and four short standalone pieces cover the full range of her formal and expressive capabilities. Two of these pieces—"Endless," from Three Movements for Percussion (1939), and "Liberty," the first movement of *Horizons* (1942)—represent some of the most astonishing music composed in the twentieth century. Kennedy and Polansky assessed this body of work as occupying "an important and almost completely overlooked place in the history of American music."[2] With their frequent focus on process rather than rhythmic complexity, Beyer's percussion works forged new territory in the genre.

Beyer composed her first work for percussion ensemble, the three-movement, thirteen-minute-long Percussion Suite, in 1933, the same year as her Quintet for Woodwinds; the Suite for Clarinet and Bassoon; Three Songs for Soprano, Percussion, and Piano; and *Sky-Pieces*. Beyer met the Seegers in 1932 and began composition lessons early that year, and the flurry of new work reflected their influence on her expansion of technique and development of new ideas. The Percussion Suite is scored for Chinese blocks, triangle, tambourine, cymbal, bass drum, xylophone, rattle, castanets, and tam-tam. The first movement is characterized by the austere, quiet plodding of the bass drum—John Kennedy writes: "It may be the first time a composer has marked percussion *sotto voce*"—which begins and ends the piece, and is constant throughout.[3] The second movement of the suite features an oft-repeated solo xylophone melody, with ever expanding intervals and frequent rhythmic variation, as well as regular use of both slow and fast glissandi, revealing Beyer's growing interest in sliding tones.[4] John Kennedy writes of Percussion Suite: "Beyer's accomplishment in the Suite is that in her first work in the genre, she immediately explored the less obvious musical parameters possible with percussion—favoring subtlety over thunder, and broadness of space and time over dense rhythm."[5]

Beyer's next percussion ensemble piece, a five-movement, approximately twelve-minute nonet titled Percussion (dated October–December 1935), has an unusual history. From the early 1940s until 2010, the entirety of this piece was unknown. The fourth movement, known as *IV*, was assumed to be a standalone piece, odd in its cryptic title, but fascinating from a performance point of view, since it was considered to be the first percussion work to leave the instrumentation and orchestration completely open—perhaps a practical decision on Beyer's part, though her previous percussion suite had been scored for specific instruments. *IV* was published in Cowell's New Music Orchestra Series No. 18 in 1936 (along with works by Doris Humphrey, Ray Green, Harold Davidson, and Gerald Strang) and remained the only work of Beyer's ever to be rendered into edited form until the publication of the piano miniature *Bees* by the Frog Peak/Johanna Beyer Project in 1996. In October 2011, in the John Cage *Notations* collection at Northwestern University, Ron Coulter found four movements by Beyer (I, II, III, and V) that clearly were the other movements to a suite—the long lost siblings of *IV*.[6] Coulter, who has studied, performed, and recorded the work, has written:

> *Percussion* is an elegant set of rhythmic studies that explore textural density. This process is enhanced by tempo variations that give the aural impression of increasing density via acceleration and decreasing density via deceleration. All five movements utilize tempo variation with indications of accelerando, ritenuto, a tempo, and allargando, with various gradations of poco, poco piu, and molto. Suspension of musical time is utilized throughout movements one, two, three, and five with fermatas occurring on measure lines. . . . What Beyer referred to as "8 times 8 measures," predates Cage's development of micro-macrocosmic rhythmic structure, albeit in a very rudimentary form. . . . Beyer's copious use of tempo variation is remarkable given the historic function of percussion instruments in pan-European art music as establishing or reinforcing the rhythmic reference point (i.e. pulse) of a composition.[7]

Considered by many to be both daring and enigmatic, *IV* still is striking in its conception—the piece is like tidal movement, constantly in motion, increasing and decreasing in both speed and volume throughout. The layering of the parts also creates an unusual visual symmetry, perhaps the reason Cowell chose it instead of the other movements for publication in his series.

All composed in 1939, Beyer's Waltz, March for 30 Instruments, and Percussion Opus 14, like the Three Movements for Percussion, were inspired by John Cage's establishment of a percussion ensemble at the Cornish School one year prior. Yet there is no evidence that the three shorter pieces were ever performed. Beyer's Three Movements for Percussion—the three movements titled "Restless," "Endless," and "Tactless"—is in some ways Beyer's most radical work. Dedicated to Cage and intended for performance by the John Cage Percussion Players in Seattle, Cage's group performed the work on at least six occasions between 1939 and 1942 in Seattle, Monterey, Moscow (Idaho), Walla Walla, Mills College in Oakland, and San Francisco.[8]

"Restless" is an almost perfect palindrome (in terms of the overall material, but at the measure level everything is always played "frontwards"), opening with an aggressively loud gong stroke played three times, with the material doubling back on itself at M. 58 and then speeding to its close with a steady accelerando. Similar arch forms occur in many of Beyer's pieces. Notated in 3/4, the middle part of the piece pits four against three to complicate the otherwise waltz-like feel. "Endless" is radical in both its form and its sound world. An insistently repeated, static woodblock pulse, swelling with small hairpin crescendi and decrescendi every two measures, is occasionally punctuated by a cymbal, repeated accents, or other increasingly ornamented embellishments at the end of each phrase cycle. A seventy-bar section is then repeated in its entirety, closed by a short coda. The relentless ("endless") tapping of the woodblock, like the ominous ticking of a clock in the middle of the night, coupled with frequent fermatas and silences, the muffled bass drum, bright cymbal, and ominous lion's roar create a kind of sonic fever dream. The courageously radical nature of the sparse texture, the minimal material, the intense focus on repetitions and small detail (the slightly changed embellishments that punctuate the phrases) foreshadow both Cage's interest in silence as a musical parameter and the minimalist idea of music as a gradual process. The third movement establishes a kind of groove characterized by each instrument focusing on one repeated motive. Gradual tempo and amplitude changes give shape to the overall form of the piece.

The other short percussion pieces Beyer composed in 1939 all included specified instrumentation and tend to be scored for approximately seven players.

March for 30 Percussion Instruments seems to have an ironic title: the meter is 4.5/4 (counted as 9/8), which would only allow for a "march" with a limp. What John Kennedy calls a "hiccupped theme" is "gradually filled in both rhythmically and by a groaning lion's roar, with bursts of forte contrasting with the baseline soft volume."[9] Percussion Opus 14 is one of only three extant pieces of Beyer's that carry opus numbers, and it is unclear why, let alone why the number is fourteen (the other two, Symphonic Opus 3 and Symphonic Opus 5, were composed around the same time, in 1939 and 1940, respectively). The piece is in 3/4 throughout and uses the acceleration-deceleration/crescendo-decrescendo pattern typical of many of her other pieces. Beyer completed another percussion work at the end of 1939, which had turned out to be a very prolific year for her. Waltz, though scored in 3/4 as would be expected, emphasizes three-against-four cross rhythms. Kennedy writes: "The work features 'rolled' downbeats through the ensemble in several instruments from low to high, creating a lovely arrhythmic wash of color underneath the interplay."[10]

Beyer composed two more percussion works before her health deteriorated. The score of *Strive*, a five-minute work for fifteen instruments played by approximately eight players, bears the date of July 1941—just one month after the last dated correspondence from Beyer to Cowell. Beyer's *Strive* appears to have been "composed on a whim" for John Cage, who had been soliciting new percussion works for a concert he wanted to hold at Mills College on July 26 of that year.[11] The piece's many tempo changes are consistent with Beyer's earlier percussion work. The use of stretched and suspended time contrasts with other percussion music of the time, as does the reduced material, and the gradual changes in texture and dynamics. Coulter points out that "texture is an integral compositional element in *Strive*, consisting of a spectrum from individual sounds framed in silence to the blurring of individual sounds by dense aggregates of sound."[12]

Beyer's last piece for percussion ensemble, composed in 1942, is also her longest and most ambitious. The sixteen-minute, four-movement *Horizons* is scored for fourteen instruments written on independent lines. No specific instrumentation is given, except for some general register distinctions. The last movement calls for "wind, water, and bird," presumably instructing the musicians to somehow reproduce those sounds in performance. The four titled movements—"Liberty," "Utopia," "Destruction," and "Reality"—are reminiscent of some of the monumental, dramatic life-themes suggested by Beyer's opera proposal *Status Quo*. Each movement has brief performance instructions as well as a short bit of poetry. This programmatic association is unique in Beyer's percussion work, though she makes extensive use of her own texts in her songs and choral pieces. The through-

Horizons, for percussion ensemble, manuscript title page; held in the John Cage Notations Collection, Northwestern University.

composed first movement "Liberty," in particular, matched the steady intensity of Beyer's earlier experiment in calm elongation of musical time in "Endless."

The performance instructions and poetic texts for *Horizons* are as follows:

I. *Liberty* (a planless "free for all") "Sleepers, toiling with a minute, with a grain of soil, poor forgotten creatures . . ."
use low pitched instruments
to give a mystic, rather subconscious impression
do the whole thing behind a curtain, if possible

II. *Utopia* ("... Behold the hypocrite, the pleasure loving, his heavenly abode ..."
use high pitched instruments
"rootless unreality"

III. *Destruction* "... Alas, fate strides in, mowing, plowing, ... purifying ..."
use all instruments
double up parts to vary the pitch
don't keep within rhythm literally
use all possible sounds and blitz tricks
vary it with each performance instinctively

IV. *Reality* ("... Stars, moon, suns, boundless beauty ...")
Sunrise
nothing is to be taken literally
with increasing intensity following a day's activities
slowly back to its starting point
Sunset

It is noteworthy that the poetic texts accompanying "Liberty" and "Reality" were taken from the texts for Beyer's own Three Songs for Soprano and Clarinet written in 1934, specifically from the song called "Universal-Local."[13] I am unaware of any other instances of Beyer "borrowing" her own material in this manner.

On July 11, 1942, Beyer wrote to Lou Harrison about *Horizons*; she was hoping he would arrange a performance in California:

> I was very happy to get your letter and enclosures about the concert. Arthur Cohn from the Philadelphia Library would like to have a copy of the program or rather a program for his files. John Cage used to send me a few and I sent it on to Cohn. He also wants the score for copying purpose. However, I would rather leave it with you now, since you have the intention to perform *Horizons* this fall, unless you make a copy of it yourself this summer. The original could be sent on. In a way it would be good to send it on to Cohn as soon as possible as all these WPA projects are very uncertain now. But again it may be best to wait till you have a chance to try it out and plan it for definite instruments. Also, coming back to performance, I begin to like the idea that a voice should utter the words belonging to each movement first before the movement itself is played. I have in mind to write a symphonic work using the same idea.[14]

Two days later, due to her increasing immobility and difficulty climbing stairs, Beyer moved from her residence of approximately six years at 40 Jane Street in Greenwich Village to the place that would be her last Manhattan address, a ground-floor apartment on Eleventh Street. Though she wrote no further percussion pieces, it is astonishing that Beyer was optimistically planning a new work for orchestra at the time.

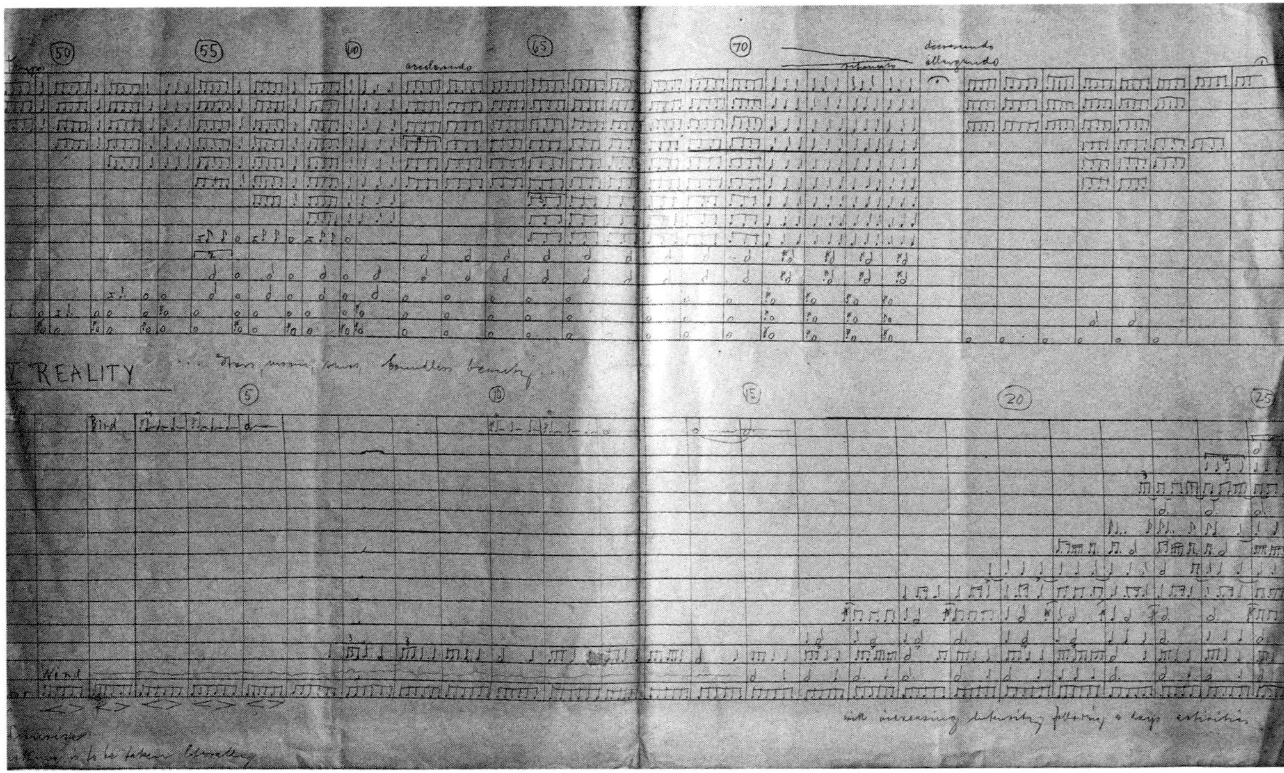

Horizons, for percussion ensemble, movement IV, "Reality," excerpt; held in the John Cage Notations Collection, Northwestern University.

6 *The People, Yes*

Songs and Choral Works

BEYER'S ENTIRE OUTPUT FOR VOICE—songs and choral works—was composed between 1933 and 1937. Her three single songs and two three-song sets make use of her own poetry and that of two other writers (see Appendix E for Beyer's original poetry.) Beyer's earliest songs reveal the influence of Ruth Crawford, whom Beyer met in early February 1932. Beyer's composition lessons with the Seegers might have continued until they moved to Washington, D.C., in late 1935. Crawford's settings of Sandburg's work, in particular her *Three Songs to Poems by Carl Sandburg* (for contralto, oboe, piano, and percussion with optional orchestral ostinati; 1930–1932) clearly influenced Beyer's choice of Sandburg's poems "Sky-Pieces," "Timber Moon, "Stars, Songs, Faces," and "Summer Grass," as well as the unusual instrumentation for her own Three Songs—soprano, piano, and percussion.[1] But as an immensely popular poet at the time, and one connected to the socialist and populist ideology embraced by Beyer's friend Bertha Reynolds and other activists in Sunnyside in the early 1930s, Sandburg might have appealed to the budding composer anyway. Beyer's manuscripts of *Sky-Pieces* are accompanied by four different cover pages, three of which reproduce, in Beyer's hand, Sandburg's quirky poem about fedoras, slouch and panama hats, derbies, and sombreros. It ends with the lines: "Hats are sky-pieces; hats have a destiny/wish your hat slowly; your hat is you."[2]

According to Beyer's 1937 CV, her three Sandburg songs were performed at the New School on October 25, 1933, in Cowell's class on contemporary American music (see chapter 2). We might speculate that Beyer was at the piano and Cowell played the percussion parts. All three pieces call for Chinese blocks, triangle, cymbal, and bass drum. The vocal parts might have been sung by Radiana Pazmor, who had performed some of Crawford's Sandburg songs at the New School around this time.[3] The second song, "Summer Grass," gives three different tempi at the start: 8th=176; 8th=160; 8th=144. It is unclear what this is supposed to mean; they might be tempo ratios (11:10:9) related to Cowell's Rhythmicana idea. This unusual song also includes *Sprechstimme* (notes "to be spoken" rather than sung, marked with x), and at the end Beyer instructs the singer: "going very gradually into a hum with closed lips going gradually from hum into ending."

Beyer's next song, *Ballad of the Star-Eater* (1934), was based on a poem by (Alice) Bonaro Wilkinson Overstreet, wife of Harry Allen Overstreet, then chair of the Philosophy Department at the City College of New York (during the 1920s and 1930s Overstreet also taught in the continuing education program at the New School for Social Research, where Beyer may have first met him). It is unclear whether or not Wilkinson Overstreet wrote the poem especially for Beyer. Beyer set the poem for soprano and clarinet, perhaps intending the high registers to represent the poem's emphasis on height and the act of climbing to the stars. This longer song setting is Beyer's only narrative work. Wilkinson Overstreet had recently published a book called *The Poetic Way of Release* (1931), which argued for the psychological power of verse, including communal poetry reading and speaking choirs.[4] The Overstreets' advocacy movement in adult education and mental health, which linked literary art and psychological theory, might have been a strong influence on Beyer, who had written a number of poems since 1932, several of which would soon be used in her other songs and choral works. The Overstreets were also friends of Bertha Reynolds, who noted their marriage in her diary on September 22, 1932.

Even today, the combination of soprano and clarinet is rare. Perhaps due to her acquaintance with the Boston Symphony Orchestra principle clarinetist Rosario Mazzeo, Beyer wrote two solo clarinet suites (1932) and a total of four songs for soprano and clarinet (1934), as well as a suite for clarinet and bassoon (1933), a sonata for clarinet and piano (1936; dedicated to Mazzeo and Nicolas Slonimsky), and a suite for bass clarinet and piano (1936?). In addition, she wrote three chamber works for woodwinds that included clarinet. For *The Ballad of the Star-Eater* Beyer might have chosen this combination because of the similar ranges of the clarinet and the average soprano. Beyer certainly would have been attracted to the clarinet's natural ability to produce sliding tones (notated by Beyer as wavy lines or arrows) and trills, as well as its relative ease in articulating disjunct melodic lines. The clarinet part starts out in a relatively low range but moves higher as the narrative turns to the collecting of stars. At a section marked *agitato molto*, the *Sprechstimme* technique is indicated by Xs. The soprano's highest note is a high G# on the word "crown." The writing is in the dissonant counterpoint style and also reflects the heterophonic interweaving of independent voices favored by Ruth Crawford. The clarinet introduction represents a structural plan Marguerite Boland calls chromatic completion or accumulation.[5] The piece is unified, with melodic material and motives returning and developing throughout. The song is about hunger, creativity, and strength, opening with the lines "Hunger assailed me with sharp, cold pain/I had searched for food, and searched in vain." After the protagonist has scaled "the wall of the sky," the song ends with this affirmation: "Now I walk the earth without care, though roots elude me and boughs are bare/ For stars still prickle my fingertips, and the taste of stars is warm on my lips/I fear no hunger with sharp, cold pain/if it dare assail me, I shall climb again."

Also composed in 1934, Beyer's Three Songs for Soprano and Clarinet are settings of Beyer's own poetry. Two of the poems ("Total Eclipse" [August] and "Universal-Local" [July]) had been written in 1932, and the third ("To Be") was dated December 1934. The pieces were performed by Mazzeo in Boston on January 29, 1936, and on a Composers' Forum-Laboratory concert on May 20, 1936.

The musical material of "Total Eclipse," with its long, dramatic text, is unified by the repeated-note ("short-long") clarinet motive that opens the piece. This is picked up by the soprano when she enters with the declaration of "moving of masses." For the 1936 Composers' Forum-Laboratory program, Beyer wrote the following: "'Total Eclipse', here I use the same tonal material for both voice and instrument, yet different rhythmical patterns. There is often imitation by the voice or vice versa, but in the development the themes vary so, that they become truly dissonant counterpoint." The beginning and ending of the song emphasize a more static, speech-like melodic pattern, while the middle of the piece rises in excitement, leading from the initial stirring of "astro-phenomena" to the goal of "phenomenous climax!" "To Be" is shorter and scored in an antiphonal (call and response) texture, with the clarinet playing increasingly elaborate flourishes between each phrase of text. (At the most virtuosic moment, the clarinetist has to play eighteen sixteenth notes within a 6/8 bar with the eighth note equaling 152.) About "To Be," Beyer wrote: "Here I also start using the same tonal material for both voice and instrument, but in entirely different rhythms and developments." "Universal-Local" is similarly brief and is tightly focused on an economical use of ideas. Here the clarinet is set very high and plays only five pitches throughout, in a consistent order and pattern, perhaps representing the repetitious regularity of the "universal." Beyer wrote: " [In] *Universal-Local*, the clarinet part keeps repeating a simple austere motive, just changing into a faster rhythmical pattern in part 2. I tried to get the never changing, sublime, universal atmosphere." *Sprechstimme* enhances the doom of "poor, forgotten creatures." This song is radical in its static sparseness and thematic conviction, "as spine-tingling as it is restrained."[6]

Beyer's last solo song, the remarkable *Have Faith!* (1936; rev. 1937), is also her most personal. Composed just a few months after Cowell's arrest, her text might refer to her feelings for him and to her effort to stay positive about the future. The song was written for flute and soprano, and dedicated to Ethel Luening, a singer married to the composer Otto Luening, who also was a flutist. The piece is short, very high, and dramatic in its declamations. The manuscript exists in three versions: one in 3/4, one in 2/4, and one in 5/8. Two of the versions require the singer to vocalize without words for some of the time—one version, composed around January 1937, included a forty-measure solo vocalization without text. In all three versions, *Sprechstimme* is used on the first iteration of the words "it does not matter."

Between 1935 and 1937 Beyer wrote five choral works: *The Robin in the Rain*, *The Federal Music Project*, *The Composers Forum-Laboratory*, *The People, Yes*, and *The Main-Deep*. *The Federal Music Project* and *The Composers Forum-Laboratory* used original texts by Beyer; both of these works were dedicated to Ashley Pettis, the director of the Composers' Forum-Laboratory. *The Robin in the Rain* set a poem by Charles Coke Woods; *The People, Yes* used a Carl Sandburg poem; and *The Main-Deep* was based on a poem by James Stephens.[7] Three of the five pieces were labeled "to the Choral Contest Committee, Federal Music Project, 254 W. 54th Str. NY."[8] Most of Beyer's choral works are for four-part, a cappella chorus; there is no evidence that any of them were performed during her lifetime.

During fall 1935, when Beyer composed her first choral work, *The Robin in the Rain* (October 1935), the Composers' Forum-Laboratory was established as part of the Music Education Division of the WPA Federal Music Project. Beyer clearly hoped to use the new opportunities to have works performed. As far as I am aware, at the time of this writing, the piece has yet to receive a premiere. *The Robin in the Rain* exists in two manuscript versions: the first, for soprano and alto chorus and a solo soprano, plus a simple, purely chordal piano part; the second version (the one dedicated to the Choral Contest Committee) is for full chorus with the same soprano solo as in the first version; the tenors and basses here take on the role of the piano drone. The piece is in three strophic verses, with the same music for each verse. In both versions the altos sing the repeated word "drop" in an onomatopoetic hocket pattern with the soprano melody, which is scalar. The solo soprano sings "the robin, the robin" on a motive that emphasizes the tritone.

Beyer's next choral piece, *The Federal Music Project*, is dated July 1936, the same month she composed her String Quartet No. 2, and the month Cowell entered San Quentin. The work is scored for four-part chorus, but the basses sing mostly a tremolo on a low F/G-flat minor second. (Based on the evidence of this piece and *The Robin in the Rain*, and given that all her solo songs were for soprano, one might speculate that Beyer was reluctant to write for male voices.) Perhaps intended as a form of populist *Gebrauchsmusik*, or music that served a certain purpose within society (as opposed to art music, that served no practical purpose), *The Federal Music Project* celebrates its titular honoree with Beyer's optimistic five-verse, strophic poem (see Appendix E).

Beyer's slow, quiet, pulsing music for *The Federal Music Project* is in some ways incongruous with this exuberant text; as the basses establish their secundal drone, the upper voices repeat the words "I know" in cascading imitation. When the basses take over the text, Beyer requests "clear diction, almost speech" as the other parts take over the drone role. After a short, imitative passage that moves up from the basses through the tenors, altos, and sopranos, Beyer creates an intriguing sonic effect in which the full chorus arrives together on an open fifth on A (coinciding with the last word of each verse): the sopranos hold the high A as the altos and tenors drop out abruptly, while the basses slide over an octave down to the low F that is the root of their drone. Each verse ends (and begins) with the plaintive repetition of "I know. . . ." Beyer's setting of *The Federal Music Project* is radical in its austerity and minimal use of thematic material.

In January 1937 Beyer set another of her own texts in a new choral work as active, humorous, and extroverted as *The Federal Music Project* had been static, contemplative, and introverted. The new piece, titled *The Composers Forum-Laboratory*, self-consciously pointed to the venue that would provide almost the only two occasions for her to hear her own work performed during her lifetime. Like its predecessor, *The Composers Forum-Laboratory* was dedicated to Pettis; it was scored for full chorus and a piano playing a bouncy, oscillating octave pattern throughout. The choral parts are mostly in imitative polyphony, and again, to her syllabic writing she adds "with clear diction," though the polyphonic layering is sometimes so dense that it obscures the words. Beyer's text is a tongue-in-cheek comment on the public-critique nature of the audience discussions following each Forum-Laboratory concert. Perhaps this poking fun at the pretentious seriousness of the Forums was not appreciated by the Choral Contest Committee.

The Main-Deep, chorus, excerpt; manuscript held in the Music Division, New York Public Library for the Performing Arts.

In September and October 1937, Beyer composed two more choral pieces. The first, *The People, Yes*, was based on Carl Sandburg's poem of the same name, which was verse 106 in a three-hundred-page book-length poem called *The People Speak* (1936). Beyer wrote out verse 106 on the cover of her manuscript. Scored for SATB a cappella chorus, the slow-moving pace of the long-held, tied and/or repeated whole notes sets the mood for the text, which begins with the line: "Sleep is a suspension midway and a conundrum of shadow lost in meadows of the moon." The staggered entries create an almost canonic pattern that results in a cluster-like sound mass. A refrain on the vocables "ai! ai!" are notated with Xs, which Beyer again explains as meaning "spoken, yet within pitch."

The Main-Deep, Beyer's last known work for chorus (a cappella SATB), was also intended for the Choral Contest Committee. Beyer hand-copied James Stephens's three-verse poem *The Main Deep* onto the cover page of her manuscript.[9] The poem is non-narrative and focuses on free-association-type word pairings that must have appealed to Beyer's elliptical and poetic sensibility ("long-rolling, steady-pouring, deep-trenched, green billow"; or later: "cold-flushing, -on-on-on-, chill-rushing, hush-hushing, hush-hushing . . ."). Beyer makes good use of words suggestive of particular treatments, especially the glissando-evocative words "pouring," "rolling," and "sliding," which are subjected to ascending or descending vocal slides usually about the distance of a major sixth (she writes in the score: "all intervals should be reached by sliding as subtle as possible!"). Beyer uses the word "hushing" (and "flushing") throughout as percussive contrast to the sliding tones and long-held notes (she notes: "the consonants 'sh' should be held and sounded"). This is Beyer's densest work in terms of chromatic layering. As a result, it is also one of her most radical in terms of sound: all the parts sing throughout, creating fullness of sound, in contrast to the thinner textures, layered imitation, and frequent structural breaks of her other choral pieces.

7 Sonatas, Suites, and String Quartets

Chamber Music

BEYER COMPOSED AT LEAST EIGHTEEN instrumental chamber works and eleven pieces for symphony orchestra or large ensemble. The clarinet was a main focus for Beyer, perhaps because of her acquaintance with Rosario Mazzeo (E-flat and bass clarinetist with the Boston Symphony Orchestra from 1933 to 1966), for whom she wrote several pieces. Though it is unclear how Beyer came to know Mazzeo, he obviously appreciated her work. He performed her Three Songs for Soprano and Clarinet in Boston and New York in 1936, recorded two movements of the Suite for Clarinet and Bassoon for New Music Quarterly Editions in 1938, and continued playing the latter work with his Crown Chamber Players in California between 1966 and 1976.[1]

Beyer's two suites for solo clarinet, composed in 1932, are landmark works of dissonant counterpoint and modernist formalism. Both are in four movements (Suite for Clarinet I: Presto, Largo, Moderato, and Rallentando; Suite for Clarinet IB: Giocoso, Lamentation, Contrast [Sonnet form], and Accelerando). The pieces are unusual in their appearance: individual lines of music ending where the phrases end (using a phrase structure technique adopted from Seeger), thus creating irregular, sometimes symmetrical lengths of systems. Beyer's "cumulation-reduction" idea (in the words of Marguerite Boland) allows her to make use of palindromes, as in the first movement of the first suite.[2] In other pieces the cumulation-reduction process manifests itself through a gradual increase or decrease in the density of orchestral textures, gradual tempo changes, dynamic swells, and repetition/alteration of material. These early clarinet pieces also reveal Beyer's engagement with dissonant counterpoint.[3] About the first suite, Boland writes, "Beyer uses an approach common to many composers working systematically with chromatic saturation or aggregate completion: the last pitch that completes the chromatic collection also signals the end of a section or movement."[4] In other words, Beyer lets pitch dictate form, carrying out systems to their logical conclusions.

The third movement of the second suite is titled "Contrast" with a subtitle in parentheses: "Sonnet form eighth=96." It is unclear what she meant by sonnet form, though the measure lengths of the twelve phrases might be thought of as a kind of metaphorical rhyme scheme: 5+7, 5+7, 5+7, 5+7, 8, 10, 9, 11. The last movements of each clarinet suite—both marked accelerando—are particularly interesting both historically and theoretically. They use another formal design written about by Cowell, namely that of "tempo melody," or a proportional rate of tempo change based on the relationship between the end of one line and the beginning of the next, a technique later called "metric modulation."[5] (Beyer writes in the score "m=m" as an abbreviation for measure=measure.) The clarinet suites are compositionally intricate and virtuosic in their demands. These are important in their theoretical implications, and they started Beyer down a path of writing a number of pieces for woodwinds.[6]

Beyer's Quintet for Woodwinds had been scheduled for performance on the May 19, 1937, Composers' Forum-Laboratory concert but was cut from the program due to time constraints. Beyer had written the following notes for the performance, and they appeared in the program:

> Quintet for Woodwinds is written in dissonant counterpoint. A dissonant chord is the signal for the discussion, the individual utterances of all participating instruments. Although only one or two instruments are heard in the beginning, they soon all talk at the same time. In the middle section one instrument after another is heard above the others in a short statement, while the rest subdue their voices. Soon they are all off again. The bassoon starts and ends the composition.

Another of Beyer's earliest known compositions, the Suite for Clarinet and Bassoon (1933; also called Suite III for Clarinet and Bassoon) holds a special place in her catalog. It was one of the first of her pieces to be performed in public and the only piece to be recorded (albeit only partially) during her lifetime. In an undated letter to Harrison Kerr, Beyer provided the following liner notes for the recording:

Suite for Clarinet I, fourth movement; manuscript held in the Music Division, New York Public Library for the Performing Arts.

II Lentamente and IV Allegretto ponderoso are parts of a Suite for Clarinet and Bassoon by Johanna Magdalena Beyer, in which an attempt is made to exhaust all possibilities in melody-writing.

II The Clarinet sings in slow motion while the bassoon runs along merrily in countermelody, counter rhythm. The passing consonances and dissonances are of secondary importance.

IV The Clarinet presents two themes in Rondo-form: The first spreads itself over space ponderously in wide skips, intervals, the second runs adjustingly up and down the gamut in close steps. All the while the Bassoon gasps humorous comments—spiced with biting wit—at such extreme emotions of it's [*sic*] partner!

But please, before you start listening to the two movements, forget all about these remarks here: Let the music speak to you directly.

The *San Francisco Examiner* allegedly reviewed the 1934 California concert as a "doleful dull duet"; but Lou Harrison later recalled the recording as "hypnotizing, a very strange and a wonderful piece."[7] Aaron Copland reviewed the recording ambivalently in *Modern Music*, an important new music journal of the time:

[New Music Quarterly Recordings] has also put on a single disc two movements [Lentamente; Allegro Ponderoso] from a Suite for clarinet and bassoon by Johanna Beyer, and Two Chorales and Ostinato for oboe and piano by Henry Cowell. Miss Beyer's pieces produce an improvisatory impression which tends to leave one suspended in mid-air. This is less true, however, of the second of the two movements.[8]

Bertha Reynolds mentioned the piece twice in her diary. On November 30, 1937, she wrote, "[J] has to pay $100 to have recordings made of her comp. by Bst. Symph. Players." More than a year later (December 8, 1938), while on a business trip to St. Louis, Reynolds reported: "Johanna's recording came. Sounds horrid." It is unclear whether she found the piece or the performance "horrid," and/or whether Beyer shared her opinion about the final product. For the 1937 Composers' Forum concert, Beyer offered these notes:

The first movement is written around the motive [dotted 8th-16th]. It occurs again and again, reversed, extended, doubled, repeated in succession, until finally the movement becomes intoxicated with the dotted rhythm which goes faster and faster in dotted sixteenths. In the second movement the bassoon takes the faster part, while the clarinet moves on slowly. The third movement contains a systematic occurrence of rests in the clarinet part. The fourth movement has two themes for the clarinet. While the main theme skips in wide tonal intervals, the second runs off in small close steps. Both are repeated and developed in rondo form. Against this is an organized rest period for the bassoon.

Beyer's Suite for Oboe and Bassoon, dated June 1939, exists in several versions with different titles, and, perhaps out of exasperation at not being able to get her pieces performed, she allowed for substitutions, writing on the score: " . . . or any other suitable instrumentation." The four-movement suite plays with modal and tonal harmonies, two-voice polyphony, chromaticism, and tunefulness. The Six Pieces for Oboe and Piano, also dated June 1939, opens with a tonal melody that sounds like quoted material. The piano part has a few clusters but mostly the piece sounds more conventional than much of her music; repeated notes, square rhythms, and a more periodic sense of phrasing make this piece unusual in her output. The second movement is static, sparse, and dark, and the two instruments never play together.

Beyer composed only two duos for strings and piano: Movement for Double Bass and Piano (1936) and Suite for Violin and Piano (January 1937). There is no evidence that the bass piece was performed during Beyer's lifetime; the Suite for Violin and Piano was performed by Beyer and violinist Carmela Ippolito at the Composers' Forum-Laboratory concert in May 1937.

The Movement for Double Bass and Piano is a good example of Beyer's interest in thematic unity and her manipulation of a reduced amount of musical material.[9] The piece starts with a nine-measure bass solo, which focuses on a repeated motive—a descending minor third, first plucked, then bowed—followed by a short chromatic melody that introduces a second, more rhythmically oriented motive (dotted-eighth, sixteenth note, quarter note; or "long-short-long"). The piano repeats this material, embellishing the original motive with clustery minor seconds in the right hand and octaves in the left. At measure 50 the bass has a cadenza-like solo that begins with a trill and then emphasizes minor seconds. The solo ends dramatically, with several one-and-a-half-octave descending glissandi. The piece ends as ominously as it began, with the austere pizzicato minor third. Why Beyer chose to write for this unusual instrumentation is unknown; perhaps she was familiar with Serge Koussevitzky's *Chanson triste* (1906), also for double bass and piano (Koussevitzky himself was an accomplished bass player). Robert Carl, in his liner notes for bassist Robert Black's recording of the piece, writes that "[the piece] is relentlessly probing and intense in the spirit of the American Ultramodernists."[10]

Beyer's equally "probing and intense" Suite for Violin and Piano, though comprising three short movements, is likewise grounded by thematic unity, tight organization, the haunting use of repeated notes, and motives brought back as if out of memory. Optimistically dedicated to Hungarian-American violinist Joseph Szigeti and the Russian-Swiss pianist Nikita Magaloff (neither of whom ever played it), the piece was premiered at the May 20, 1937, Composers' Forum-Laboratory concert, with Beyer at the piano. She offered these notes:

> The violin states the theme out of which the whole material for the Suite derives, tonally and rhythmically. The second measure of the 4/4 rhythm theme has only three quarter notes instead of four. These three notes become very significant. In the first movement they appear insistently in the piano part against the 4/4 beat of the violin, while in the second movement the three beats of the violin throb against the four of the piano. In the first [*sic*: third] movement these three beats occur again in the piano part. Violin and piano take alternatively one motive of the theme and comment on it, resulting in abstraction.

Beyer favored this polyrhythmic play of four-against-three for creating tension between instruments. The short cadenza that opens the third movement reiterates melodic ideas found in the solo opening of the first movement. The piece, like the Movement for Double Bass and Piano, reveal a dark, brooding quality in Beyer's writing. Following the 1937 premiere of the piece, for which there was apparently a "good-sized audience," the *New York Herald-Tribune* described this piece as "experimental in form and modernistic in harmony."[11]

Beyer's four works for string quartet make a sizable contribution to the twentieth-century repertoire for that ensemble: String Quartet (1933–34); String Quartet No. 2 (July 1936); Movement for String Quartet (also called *Dance for Strings*; 1938); and String Quartet IV (undated). A "String Quartet No. 3" has not been found; Beyer possibly counted the Movement for String Quartet as the third in this series of four works for quartet.

The first quartet, like the second and fourth, is set in a classical four-movement form: Allegro; Lento; Moderato; and Presto. Written in the year following Beyer's initial composition lessons with the Seegers, it would be difficult to deny the influence of Ruth Crawford's String Quartet (1931), which included not only virtuosic displays of dissonant counterpoint but also featured one of the most radical (and earliest) uses of a completely static sound-mass texture. Beyer clearly had studied Crawford's work; its form, compositional techniques, and sound world are reflected especially in Beyer's first two quartets.

The first quartet's Presto movement, in particular, seems modeled on the groundbreaking third movement of Crawford's quartet. Playing with mutes, and asked to play the softest pianissimo possible (*con sordini ppp sempre ppp*), the strings whisper through a landscape of glissandi, sliding tones, slight swells in dynamics. Polansky describes this movement:

> The fourth movement is nothing short of astonishing. In its minimalist use of material, and focus on timbre and gesture, it might have been written fifty years later (listen for the second violin repeating a high E-flat half-note pulse for one hundred and twenty-nine measures). It is a unified, fantastic sound world, almost completely composed of glissandi, crescendi/

decrescendi clusters, and few somewhat surprising "melodies" near the end. Its closest aesthetic relative may be another Beyer piece, *The Federal Music Project*.[12]

Near the end of the movement, all the parts slide down to an F-E double-stop on the second violin: the E eventually drops out, and the piece ends with a long decrescendo on the lone F. Beyer's way of notating some of the slides and fades foreshadow the radical graphic notation of the 1960s in the music of composers like Krzysztof Penderecki and George Crumb.

The four movements of Beyer's String Quartet No. 2—Allegretto, Largo, Moderato, and Allegro quasi Presto—reveal again the influence of Crawford, especially in Beyer's Largo, which likewise recalls the third movement of Crawford's String Quartet. But the piece also reflects similarities to Ives's playful settings of tonal quotations in atonal contexts. Beyer's first and last movements both use the melody from a well-known aria in Mozart's *Die Zauberflöte* (*The Magic Flute*): Papageno's "Ein Mädchen oder Weibchen. . . ." The aria, the first to be heard in the opera, establishes the lead character of Papageno as hungry for a "girl or a wife."[13] The upbeat, tonal tune is played by the cello in both instances; in the first movement other parts play fragments of it as well. It is framed by sliding tones, drawing attention to the contrast between a lyrical melody and the abstract textures of modernism.[14]

The Movement for String Quartet (or, *Dance for Strings*) is somewhat unusual in its instrumentation: violin, viola, cello, and double bass. Written two years after her Movement for Double Bass and Piano, Beyer might have been interested in writing solo material again for bass. This 221-measure movement has probably never been performed. An opening section focuses on a static texture on D with a pulse in the viola; the instruments enter *forte* and then fade to *piano*. This dramatic, fading gesture is then repeated. After a meter and tempo change, a dance-like melody appears in the viola with the cello and bass accompanying lightly, the violin plays a countermelody. The piece seems less radical than much of Beyer's music, with a steady pulse, thin texture, and transparent, repetitive themes throughout. The static fade on D returns to close the piece in a rounded way.

Beyer's undated String Quartet IV might have been her last piece. It is written in clear handwriting that looks like perhaps someone else copied it. The first movement Moderato has no tempo marking, is set in 4/4, and is in C major. The first violin plays a repeated melody that sounds like a quotation of the third phrase in "Freres Jacques"—the part in English that sings: "Morning bells are ringing! Morning bells are ringing!" The cello plays an oscillating line that resembles the beginning of the requiem mass chant "Dies Irae," or "Day of Wrath." At

String Quartet No. 2, fourth movement, excerpt; manuscript held in the Music Division, New York Public Library for the Performing Arts.

measure 62 the cello is stranded on triplet low Es for the rest of the movement. The Larghetto bears the mark of dissonant counterpoint in that it seems to be a study in contrast. The third movement Andante is thin-textured and austere, and makes interesting use of chromaticism, recalling Shostokovich's dark contrast of major and minor and his use of relentlessly repeated notes that move suddenly to something unexpected. Beyer's Presto finale also exploits both a sparse sound (the cello playing open fifths) and the compound meter's ability to emphasize duple or triple patterns at the same time. Beyer changes the key signature frequently in this piece and brings back material in reorchestrated forms. Like the Movement for String Quartet, Beyer's String Quartet IV has never been performed.

8 Symphonic Striving

Works for Band and Orchestra

BETWEEN 1935 AND 1941, Beyer wrote eleven works for large ensembles, from her nine-instrument March of 1935 to her full-orchestra Symphonic Movement II of 1941, which she dedicated, optimistically, to Leopold Stokowski. Seven of these works were for the forces of the Romantic orchestra, with enhanced percussion sections; five were copied and archived at the Edwin A. Fleisher Collection of Orchestral Music in the Free Library of Philadelphia.[1]

According to musicologist Judith Tick, the notion of a "woman composer" of orchestral music was not established until just a few decades before Beyer began composing:

> In 1893 the Boston Symphony Orchestra under the direction of Kikisch performed the Overture *Wichitis* by Margaret Lang—the first time any orchestra in the United States had performed a piece composed by an American woman. Three years later the same orchestra performed the *Gaelic Symphony* of Mrs. H. H. A. Beach—the first symphony composed by an American woman. Lang and Beach therefore established the precedent that women could indeed compose orchestral music.[2]

Following an era during which most women in music were singers, pianists, harpists, patronesses, or friends to celebrated men in the field, it is not surprising that many who remembered Beyer at all remembered her as "Cowell's secretary" rather than as a fellow composer who toiled over her orchestral scores just as they did. But she was not alone in her desire to write for larger forms, and there were a few precedents, though she may not have known them. The November 25, 1933, issue of *Musical America* featured an article titled "Works by Two Women Composers Played by Philadelphia Orchestra." Frances McCollin's *Adagio for String Orchestra* and Ione Pickhardt's *Mountains* were conducted by Stokowski, who claimed to be "continuing his search for novelties."

Beyer's March of April 1935 was completed just before her departure for Germany in May of that year, a trip that would be her last to the country of her birth. She wrote March on manuscript paper issued by the Irving Berlin Standard Music Corporation, which featured pre-printed instrumental staves, including lines for saxophones and banjo. Beyer turned the paper upside-down and ignored the predetermined instrumentation, which was probably intended for band or musical theater. The manuscript is crowded and displays what appear to be Beyer's own corrections. Beyer copied out all the parts, which included two clarinets, two cornets, cymbal and drum, two violins, and cello. It is unclear why she wrote for this particular combination. The piece is odd, given Beyer's exploration of dissonant counterpoint at the time: except for two brief passages in the cello part and one passage in the clarinet part, the entire piece consists of parallel fourths. The rhythm is regular and even, and the drum and cymbal play triplet patterns throughout.

Until recently, Beyer's *Fragment for Chamber Orchestra*, dated January 1937, was her only orchestral piece that had ever been performed. It was premiered by the Ensemble Resonanz and recorded live by Westdeutscher Rundfunk during a festival in Cologne, Germany, in 1999. This approximately six-minute piece was dedicated to Hans Lange, the violinist and, at the time of the dedication, associate conductor of the Chicago Symphony Orchestra. The piece was copied by the Fleisher Collection, but Beyer made parts herself for the chamber group consisting of flute, oboe, clarinet, bassoon, horn in F, two violins, viola, cello, double bass, piano, and percussion (Chinese blocks, cymbal, and bass drum). *Fragment*'s slow and quiet opening passages are dominated by an evocative series of solo oboe phrases, accompanied by atmospheric long tones in the muted strings and slow cluster chords in the piano. Chinese blocks play on the oboe's rests, causing a hocket-like conversation between the two dissimilar instruments. This unifying hocket theme recurs throughout. The sparse texture of the opening is joined by countermelodies in the flute and clarinet; the bassoon plays a pattern of three against the general setting of four, one of Beyer's favorite techniques for creating a feeling of tension. In the middle of the piece, the piano has an eight-bar solo passage. The last section switches to 3/4, but maintains much of the thematic material of the opening.

The cellos are given two-octave glissandi. A sudden flourish in the piano and the opening's oboe and Chinese block motive close the piece, as a last held chord in the piano slowly fades away with the oboe's final held high D. The piece, far from a mere "fragment," is beautiful and effective, and it demonstrates Beyer's sensitivity to instrumental combinations, thematic material, and formal drama.

Soon after *Fragment for Chamber Orchestra*, Beyer composed her first work for *full* orchestra, the four-movement Symphonic Suite (dated January–July 1937), which the composer estimated to be about twenty-four minutes long.[3] The movements include an opening Grave, an Allegretto scherzando, a Lentamente, and a Presto finale, marked "as fast as possible." The first movement opens similarly to *Fragment for Chamber Orchestra*, with a clarinet solo marked *espressivo*, accompanied by sparse pizzicato strings. The full orchestra that follows the introduction is mostly homorhythmic (all the parts moving together). The end of the Grave features English horn, oboe, and bassoon solos; the Allegretto scherzando begins *attacca*. This movement, too, foregrounds paired soloists: at the opening, piccolo and bassoon; at the end, piccolo and percussion. An antiphonal passage follows the opening, which sets the string section against the brass instruments in an imitative call-and-response passage. The Lentamente movement likewise emphasizes solo wind melodies while the piano plays a jarring but slow-moving series of augmented octaves (or minor ninths). Throughout, the triangle (and sometimes glockenspiel) plays a three pattern against the overall time of four. The Presto features a fast-moving 9/8 unison melody in the winds.

In February 1938, Beyer composed a piece called *Reverence* for wind ensemble (piccolo, flute, English horn, clarinet, bassoon, soprano saxophone, tenor saxophone, alto horn, "brass," euphonium, timpani, and bass drum) and dedicated it to the Australian pianist, bandleader, and composer Percy Grainger. Beyer's correspondence with Grainger seems to have begun in November 1937, after Cowell connected them. As she introduced herself to Grainger, she remarked that she had heard him conduct a piece of Cowell's (*Reel*) on the radio, broadcast from the Interlochen International Music Camp in Michigan, in August 1937. She added: "And being also a composer, I know your works of course." She enlisted him in her efforts to promote Cowell's book manuscript "The Nature of Melody," written during his early months in prison, for which Beyer sought support through publishing companies and funding agencies like Fischer, Knopf, and the Guggenheim Foundation, and for which she had "been checking up examples and the like."[4] But their correspondence was only partly about Cowell. Soon Grainger became an important channel through which Beyer could talk about her own music; clearly she craved contact with other composers and hungered for feedback and mentoring. She enjoyed discussing with Grainger the tedium of copying parts, obtaining and comparing various types of manuscript paper, and other mundane composers' trade details.[5]

Grainger also encouraged Beyer's interest in exploring new compositional idioms, supported her efforts to write for concert band and wind ensemble, and, on at least one occasion, brought these works to life.[6] In 1939 Cowell conveyed to Grainger Beyer's reaction to seeing Grainger conduct a rehearsal of her concert band and wind ensemble pieces *Reverence* and *Elation*: "She was speechless with pleasure over having had the opportunity to hear her own work rehearsed—her own statement is that she was deeply thrilled, but tried not to show it!"[7] Beyer also shared her enthusiasm with Grainger: "I really felt very grateful to you for taking all this trouble, it was really a thrill despite! . . . It was a fine experience for me, and the best lesson I could possibly have."[8] This would turn out to be the only time Beyer had the opportunity to hear any of her large ensemble pieces performed live.

Beyer's remaining orchestral works include the Symphonic Movement I, Symphonic Suites 1 and 2, the four-movement Symphonic Op. 3, the three-movement Symphonic Op. 5, and *CYRNAB*. While her Symphonic Op. 3 might be the most ambitious of these pieces, *CYRNAB* is perhaps the most interesting. As Kennedy and Polansky first pointed out, *CYRNAB* appears to be an anagram-like construction taken from the middle of the names "henRYCowell" and "johanNABeyer," implying, perhaps, something "about Beyer's perception of her relationship to Cowell."[9] Beyer composed this approximately twelve-minute piece in fall 1937, after Cowell had been sentenced and after she had begun corresponding with Grainger. It is written for a large orchestra: piccolo, flute, oboe, English horn, B-flat clarinet, bassoon, contra-bassoon, trumpet in F, horn in F, trombone in B-flat, trombone in F, tuba in F, timpani, Chinese blocks, cymbal, gong, bass drum, piano, violin 1, violin 2, viola, cello, and double bass. The piece is in two sections, 120 and 197 measures long, respectively. A *sforzando* gong stroke opens the piece, followed by a quiet, slow horn call playing repeated open fifths. When the percussion, piano, and strings enter, the texture remains thin and static. The winds likewise enter with slowly oscillating seconds, while the brass gradually add some movement. A high single pitch held in the horn provides a seamless transition to the second section. This is set in 6/8 and features the violins playing pizzicato eighth notes and the winds playing a dance-like melody that contrasts with the static calm of the opening. The piano plays chromatically moving octaves on the strong beats of one and four. Several solo phrases interrupt this pattern. The finale features much of the opening material as well as some faster flourishes and many

Symphonic Movement II, first movement, excerpt; manuscript held in the Music Division, New York Public Library for the Performing Arts.

dynamic swells. The end is a very quiet fade of the horn repeating the open fifth heard at the beginning of the piece, with the strings playing muted C-sharps.

Beyer's orchestral works raise many questions about her ambition and her expectations. She communicated with many famous conductors—including Carlos Chávez, Eugene Goossens, Howard Hanson, Hans Kindler, Otto Klemperer, Serge Koussevitzky, Karl Krueger, Hans Lange, Fritz Mahler, Pierre Monteux, Artur Rodzinski, Lazare Saminsky, Fabien Sevitzky, Nicolas Slonimsky, Leopold Stokowski, Joseph Szigeti, and Alfred Wallenstein—yet she was unable to interest any in her larger works. Koussevitzky, for one, looked at her Symphonic Suite of 1937 and deemed it "not convincing," with no further explanation.[10] Despite this lack of support, Beyer not only composed a number of substantial symphonic pieces, but she also copied individual instrumental parts for most of them. This tedious yet hopeful process must have occupied a great deal of her time. In a rare acknowledgement of her diligence, Cowell wrote Beyer some encouraging words from San Quentin on August 15, 1937: "It would be splendid, if Koussevitzky in Boston would take an interest in your new orchestral piece. It would be worth the work. I fully appreciate your hopeless feeling when engaged in copying parts!" According to a letter Beyer wrote to Lou Harrison in 1942, she "had it in mind" to write a new symphonic work, one that would include narration of some sort, similar to what she intended for her large percussion suite *Horizons*.[11] Symphonic Movement II (1941) would remain her last orchestral piece.

In the last years of her life Beyer became increasingly frustrated over her inability to generate interest in her orchestral work, and on June 4, 1941, she exasperatedly wrote to Cowell, "I ought to hear at least one work once." Sadly, she never did. On March 1, 2014, during the final stages of writing this book, I drove forty-five minutes from my home in Santa Cruz, California, with a small group of musician friends, to hear conductor John Kennedy give the world premiere of Beyer's Symphonic Movement I (1939) with the Santa Clara University Orchestra. As I listened to this piece that had been silent for seventy-five years, with the manuscript in hand, I wondered what Beyer might have learned about writing for orchestra, had she had the opportunity to hear some of these works performed during her lifetime.

9 *Status Quo*

ONE OF BEYER'S MOST AMBITIOUS PROJECTS was a plan for an opera called *Status Quo*, for which she decided to apply for a Guggenheim Foundation Fellowship in the summer of 1937.[1] Composers who won Guggenheim awards between the fellowship's establishment in 1925 and the year Beyer's proposal was submitted in 1938 included Aaron Copland (1925), Leopold Damrosch Mannes (1926), Roger Sessions (1926 and 1927), Roy Harris (1927 and 1928), Quincy Porter and Randall Thompson (both 1929 and 1930), Ruth Crawford (1930), Otto Luening (1930 and 1931), Henry Cowell (1931), George Antheil (1932 and 1933), Adolph Weiss (1932), William Grant Still (1934, 1935, and 1938), Dante Fiorillo (1935, 1936, 1937, and 1938), Walter Piston (1935), Ross Lee Finney (1937), Paul Creston (1938 and 1939), David Diamond (1938), and Carlos Chávez (1938).[2] The most frequently supported person in this group is hardly a household name today: Dante Fiorillo, a self-taught composer and undistinguished cellist, had established ties to both the Yaddo artist retreat and Black Mountain College. Ruth Crawford was the only woman composer awarded a grant during this early period (though it is also not known how many women besides Beyer applied). During the first thirty years of the fellowship's existence, it was awarded to only two other women composers: Louise Talma (1946) and Peggy Glanville-Hicks (1955). Age as well as gender may have been a factor in

Beyer's rejection: a file card documenting her proposal concluded unceremoniously: "At age 50 she doesn't appear to be a good risk as a composer." Indeed, of the twenty-seven composers awarded Guggenheim Fellowship grants between 1925 and 1938, only a handful were over forty: Adolph Weiss (41), Walter Piston (41), and William Grant Still (43 during his third Guggenheim year); the oldest fellow in the early group was Theodore J. Stearns, at age 46.

In October 1937 Beyer asked Koussevitzky and several composers to act as a reference for her proposal.[3] She sent Koussevitzky an annotated resume, which, remarkably, has remained the sole source for certain details about her life. The "work plan" she provided Koussevitzky, basically a draft of the Guggenheim project proposal itself, outlined a four-act, twelve-scene opera "that will be modern both in theme and musical form," she explained.[4] She wished to spend a year on the composition, "which, in combination with various forms of pantomimes, dances, as well as speech, exclamations, songs, would seem to express our modern life." She explained her aims: "The traditional themes of the opera are outworn and of little significance for our time. Likewise the musical form of the opera, which related itself to these older themes, is quite inadequate for the musical consciousness of our present world." (Indeed, just a few years earlier, on February 20, 1934, Virgil Thomson and Gertrude Stein's experimental *Four Saints in Three Acts* opened on Broadway, challenging the "outworn" forms of both opera and musical theater.) In an undated letter (probably 1938) Beyer wrote to Harrison Kerr excitedly of her work on the opera: "I am living a fast life here, I tell you, working like hell; the music for my *Status Quo* comes out well, I am almost crazy from all the melodies swirling around in my head, sticky ones too, people will be surprised what I can do!" In August 1938 Beyer announced to Grainger: "I have finished my *Status Quo*, a pageant to music . . ., but I have only finished a short-hand score. The real copying work has to start in now."[5] Beyer submitted her Guggenheim application in late 1938; her proposal was rejected in early 1939.[6] At present, a completed, even "short-hand score" of *Status Quo* has not been found.

Instead, we have only Beyer's detailed description of the opera and two sections of music that were intended to be part of it. Both pieces were apparently completed in or around 1938: *Music of the Spheres*, a "movement for three electrical instruments"; and *Dance*, for full orchestra, the title page of which was labeled *Status Quo, Part of Act IV: Geneva*. Though *Status Quo* was never fully realized, and none of it was ever performed—except for *Music of Spheres*, discussed separately below—it is worth considering in some detail, given that Beyer provides us with considerable information about her aesthetic intentions and also because Beyer's Guggenheim evaluations, written by prominent people who were asked to assess her proposal, contain candid and widely varying responses regarding her talent and her personality. Finally, given that Beyer intended the work to culminate in "the essence of music, derived from all existing systems," it might have constituted, had it been supported, a *Gesamtkunstwerk* extravaganza in a class with other pioneering works of musical theater written during the mid-twentieth century.

An eyewitness confirms that the ideas in *Status Quo* were of significant importance to Beyer, perhaps expressing many of the socialist and populist ideas proliferating in Sunnyside during the late 1920s and early 1930s. Composer Ray Green, who visited Beyer in her Jane Street apartment at the time she was planning the opera, later recalled:

> From her description of the piece it was political in motivation and she was quite vehement by what she thought of as the political injustice of the period in which she was living. She was very indignant about the 'status quo' as she talked to me. My impression of her was that she was a person passionately devoted to her convictions.[7]

In her Guggenheim proposal Beyer explained that she wished for the opera to be significant to the "modern age" and to the "ideas and interests that are vital in our present world." Not only the ideas but the music would be relevant to Beyer's time: "I shall also be able to recall various historical music systems and give them their significant placing in the evolution of our social life." The four acts, taking place in "the present," would have the following settings: Act I: U.S.A.; Act II: The Kremlin; Act III: Rome-Berlin; Act IV: Geneva. In her synopsis of the opera, Beyer described background screen projections ("picturing star systems, our globe, different continents . . ."), music ("all existing musical systems according to stage and screen"), and the broad events of the individual scenes. It is clear from the following summary that Beyer had not planned the later acts in much detail at the time of her Guggenheim application. The practical depiction of rapidly juxtaposed places—jumping from Schenectady, New York, to the North Pole, for example—is hard to imagine in performance. Beyer's inclusion of the fascist rallies in Nuremberg in Act III is notable, as is her apparent utopian belief in the neutrality of Switzerland in Act IV.

> *ACT I*: U.S.A.
>
> *Scene 1*: America: New York. Pair, eastern type, in subway discussion world affairs, their point of view.
>
> *Screen*: Stars, globe, America, U.S.A., airoplanes [*sic*], steamers, skyscrapers, Broadway, Harlem, Chinatown, Ghetto . . .
>
> *Music*: energetic, pulsating, syncopated, cross rhythms, dissonant counterpoint, polyphonic.
>
> *Scene 2*: Pair, western intellectuals, going across country in plane: Schenectedy [*sic*],

Washington D.C., New Deal, Mt. Wilson Observatory, San Francisco, Bay Bridge, shipping, strike, across Northpole

Screen: Schenectedy [*sic*], Washington, Lobby, Lobbyists, Northpole: icebergs, icefields, snow wastes . . .

Music: flowing, throbbing, of exultation, exuberance, American folktunes, according to screen, across Northpole just primitive percussion beats.

Scene 3: England: Abdication of Edward VIII, coronation pageant

Screen: accordingly

Music: Neoclassical, conventional

Scene 4: France:

Screen: accordingly

Music: French, Debussy, 6-tone scales

ACT II: The Kremlin

Scene 1: Russia: Moscow, all their new achievements; Syberia [*sic*]

Screen: Youth, factories, nurseries, schools, artprojects, collective farms

Music: Marches, marching songs. . . .

Scene 2: China being aggressed

Screen: accordingly

Music: oriental, using original records possibly

Scene 3: India-Africa being ruled

Screen: accordingly

Music: Hindu-African

Scene 4: Ireland

Screen: the isle, scenery . . .

Music: Gaelic, bagpipes, jigs, reels

ACT III: Rome–Berlin

Scene 1: Europe continental, Germany

Screen: Nürnberg Festival

Music: Folktunes, marches, conventional, modern

Scene 2: Italy

Screen: Rome fascist rally

Music: marches . . .

Scene 3: Spain

Screen: accordingly

Music: Spanish

ACT IV: Geneva

Scene 1: Geneva

Screen: Switzerland, peaks of eternal snow, Wilhelm Tell [?] flags and representatives of all countries

Music: essence of music, derived from all existing systems.

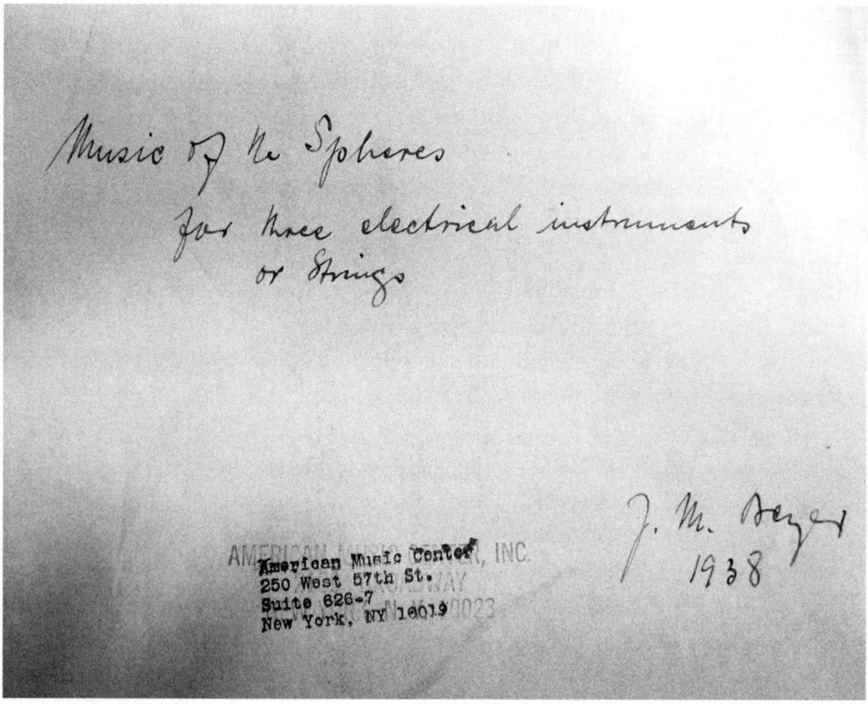

Music of the Spheres, title page; manuscript held in the Music Division, New York Public Library for the Performing Arts.

The two existing pieces of music from the opera include *Dance* for full orchestra and *Music of the Spheres*. *Music of the Spheres*, the "movement for three electrical instruments," appears to be a kind of prelude to the opening scene of *Status Quo*. The manuscript is dated July 1938, and Beyer estimates the piece to last about five minutes. The "three electrical instruments" are accompanied by a triangle that occasionally plays a short-long part throughout. What Beyer meant by "electrical" in 1938 is unclear. In the *Dance* section of Act IV, she writes for what appears to be electric cello ("El. Cello").

A short section of music written on the second page of *Music of the Spheres* seems to have been intended as an introduction to that piece. What appears to be an eleven-bar timpani pulse joined by a lion's roar is labeled "Beginning of *Status Quo*, Screen: Star systems." Immediately following is a trill played by an "electrical instrument," with the note "leading into *Music of the Spheres*." The triangle takes over the trilled minor second, and then the three sliding instruments enter one by one. The lowest voice oscillates between F and E in bass clef, the middle part plays long-held notes, and the top part is very high whole notes. A note in the score instructs "all intervals are to be taken glissando as subtle as possible." The piece starts very slowly (quarter note equals 52) and very quietly (*ppp*), but, as in much of Beyer's music, a gradual arch form occurs over time. The opening dynamic and tempo are a "starting point, gradually increasing speed and dynamics"; about halfway through the piece the tempo has reached a whole note equaling 52 (four times as fast as the opening), and she indicates "gradually decreasing speed and dynamics back to the staring point" (the whole piece is marked "Lento-Moderato-Lento"). The piece dramatically dies away with a marking of "morendo."

Beyer included in her Guggenheim application a typescript of an ambitiously cosmic introductory statement meant to be read by "Voice (Announcer)":

> Presently we will hear *Music of the Spheres*, see star systems happenings of the Universe, to remind us of eternal truth, beauty, infinity. We will see our earth, floods, vegetation, ancient animals, and some of our ancestors.
>
> On the stage two primitive creatures roam around in darkness. We hear a cry, a wail stops in response: sound and rhythm are herewith given. And in this introduction we will witness the development of these two elements into music from the very primitive to the complicated of our day.
>
> When arrived at the use of most complex rhythm, melody, harmony, we find ourselves in America, the U.S.A. And we better be prepared, for here we will experience cause and effect of complex music: life at a *Sturm and Drang* period: stress, uncertainty, the restlessness of 1938/1939. After this we will travel to other islands, continents, other climates, surroundings, circumstances and be anxious to find out, what other influences may do to music, into what our two elements, sound and rhythm have developed there.
>
> We will find, that everywhere, music is closely related to life and that there are developed in music various systems—some thousands of years old. And although this or that system of music from other countries is unfamiliar to us, we must be tolerant and interested, as we are in the lives of these different peoples, and then we will experience, that these strange sounds have a certain beauty. The understanding and joy of it will increase to the degree of our interest in it.
>
> In the last set, just before having another glimpse of eternity, people from all these countries will unite in a dance. Tolerance and cooperation will be the motives. The music to this dance is an attempt to unite features of different music systems to a rather substantial harmonious whole.
>
> And with this accomplished we will join the spheres once more.[8]

To some degree, ideas in this introduction, and in *Status Quo* in general, echo cosmic and poetic ideas Beyer explored in many of her song texts (see Appendix E), ideas she also expressed in a letter to Alvin Johnson on August 30, 1936: "Our music could not possibly be subjective. The vast stretches of our land, many-fold races, vast cities, the rhythm, pulse of our life must ultimately bring an objective, synthetic style about, to be authentic American music." In her ambitious introduction to *Status Quo*, Beyer meshed ideas from astronomy, evolution, geopolitics, and utopianism, and thereby allowed her imagination to cast a wide net for themes to stream through her opera. Her reference to the "stress, uncertainty, the restlessness" of the time allude to growing anxiety about the coming war in Europe.

Beyer's *Dance* for full orchestra, labeled *Part of Act IV: Geneva*, might have been intended as the final section of the opera, as the final section of *Dance* leads back to *Music of the Spheres*, which, as is indicated by the narration above, would appear to close the work in Beyer's preferred arch form. *Dance* is preceded by one page of music in several short sections that are unclear in their numbering and their geographical meaning, but clear in the way she intended instrumentation to depict cultural references:

10. Pair: France [a 7-bar section for musette and piano]
11. Pair: England [a 7-bar section for bagpipe and piano]
12. Pair: America [a 7-bar section for "El. cello" and piano and/or trombones]

This is followed by a short section marked "Dance—Adjustment," which continues with "El. cello," piano and trombone, and then moves to violin and viola, piano, and trombone. Similar to the "pairs" section, these short passages feature simple melodies. Then the *Dance* movement begins, for full orchestra, including piccolo, saxophone, tuba in F, contrabassoon, piano, percussion (tambourine, cymbal, snare drum, bass drum, and timpani in D), and a muted solo trumpet. After a 210-measure exploration of this rich range of orchestral color, the reprise of *Music of the Spheres* is introduced by the pulsing piano, which continues with the triangle as an ominous accompaniment to the three sliding "electric instruments." *Music of the Spheres* was composed one year before John Cage's historically celebrated *Imaginary Landscapes #1* (1939), which similarly exploited the possibilities of electric glissandi, coupled with sparse percussion and muted piano accompaniment.

Beyer's Guggenheim application file included a number of written evaluations of her proposal by experts in the field.[9] They are contradictory in that some praise her talent while others refuse to endorse her operatic ambitions. (Koussevitzky's rejection of her Symphonic Suite in connection with her Guggenheim application has been mentioned elsewhere.) Perhaps most significant is the recommendation written by (an incarcerated) Henry Cowell, given the depth and complexity of their relationship. He called her a "great natural talent . . . with a flare for whimsical and original ideas." He spoke of her "fine technique" and "good workmanship." Still, his report recommended Gerald Strang for a Guggenheim instead of Beyer. Strang, in turn, wrote an assessment of Beyer, first praising and then damning his competitor for the award: "While her music shows a good deal of originality I find it diffuse and intellectual. I am not convinced that it has much musical meaning. Hence I very much doubt her ability to carry out this project in such a way as to produce a significant contribution to musical literature." Other assessments were varyingly positive, negative, thoughtful, and dismissive. Wallingford Riegger found the proposal for *Status Quo* suggestive of *National Geographic* magazine, but in the end he determined "it would be a worthy thing for the Foundation to sponsor." Marion Bauer admitted she did not know much of Beyer's work but said that what she had seen of it, she had found "interesting." Bauer mentioned that her friend Ruth Crawford "always spoke of her as having unusual talent." Harry Overstreet "unhesitatingly" recommended Beyer—"unquestionably a first-rater." Ashley Pettis, too, felt Beyer was "a musician of excellent training and background" and added: "Her outstanding characteristics are her interest in musical innovation and her untrammeled, adventurous spirit." He wholeheartedly endorsed her proposal.

Alvin Johnson, on the other hand, with whom Beyer had much contact on Cowell's behalf during this time, wrote: "I do not think she has either the intellectual power or the command of her art to do anything with the theme she proposes." Roy Harris pompously asserted: "To create new operatic idioms is a life work requiring great talent, resourcefulness and experience with the orchestra, the voice (as solo and chorus) and experience with music in relation to the theatre." He concluded: "Such equipment I cannot honestly say that I believe Miss Beyer to be possessed of." (Apparently Beyer had her own doubts about Harris's "equipment"; on January 19, 1941, she wrote to Cowell: "Just listened to Roy Harris 3. Symphony, but am not convinced. What is he aiming at? The effects of *Finlandia*?") On the other hand, Ruth Hannas, a professor of composition at the University of North Carolina, Greensboro, wrote of Beyer's "creative gift," which she considered "authentic in its medium of expression."[10]

Most surprising in this collection is a letter from Erdix Winslow Capen, Bertha Reynolds's first cousin, who had known Beyer and her music since at least 1932, when he visited Sunnyside and Beyer played her music for him. They remained friends. Capen worked as an art instructor and a theater designer, and he wrote a passionate endorsement for Beyer's proposal, quoted in full below:

> I have known the candidate Miss Beyer for a number of years. Probably for about seven. Through visits to New York and through mutual acquaintances I have kept in touch with her and her work. We have corresponded for several years at irregular intervals. I have been

interested in her work as something rare and unique, since she first explained her beliefs and demonstrated her compositions to me. I think that she has unusual ability and a very rare and interesting way of looking at things which is apparent in her work. She seems to be way ahead of most of her contemporaries in her thoughts of music and its place in the world. She has a highly individual method of composition and thinking which make her work valuable to music and especially towards opera in which direction her thought seems at present to be turning. I am not a musician myself but am a theatre artist and technician and from such a viewpoint her music seems to have a more alive quality for the theatre than any that I have known. An opera by her should be a departure for the good, from any existing forms, judging from her past work, still without being created only in the spirit of being different. The peculiarities of her work don't spring from any desire to be different but from a truly different feeling and approach. I feel certain that given the wherewithal and the chance to work it out she will rise to heights that she has thus far been unable to reach because of lack of funds to tend to her needs while she worked. I have read the plan she has submitted. My reaction to it from her description and knowing her, is that it is a very fine idea and very good theatre and so few things labeled opera seem to have that. It has the stamp of the living on it rather than the outmoded form of a past century which is so seldom completely satisfactory at present. She seems to have hit on a vital plan for opera which is worth trying for its possibilities of future development as well as possibly releasing a new talent and giving added creative chance to a woman who has been held under too long for her own good. She has a gift for unceasing labour. She has more capacity for hard work than anyone else who has crossed my path so far. In spite of that she is not an 'ivory tower' sort of person and her work is very much in the present in thought and expression. I am thoroughly convinced from what I have heard of her work that she is as near a genius as I am ever likely to meet up with. In case you feel that I have been blowing her horn too consistently I want to say that everything I have said I firmly believe to be true. I have complete faith in her abilities as a composer and in the far reaching influence of her work. I wouldn't care to have her know that I think as highly of her work as I do but she knows that I have plenty of faith in her abilities.

This generous assessment of Beyer's creative potential from someone outside the modernist musical establishment is astounding in its detail and dedication, and perhaps is a testimony to how devoted Beyer's Sunnyside friends remained to her throughout her life. Capen's compliments contrast starkly with the derision of a privileged composer like Roy Harris, who claimed that Beyer had no experience with the orchestra, voice, or theater, even though he would not have had any authority to make such an assumption.

It is worth pointing out that two of the three women who wrote letters for Beyer gave her the benefit of the doubt (Ruth Hannas: "I am not positive she understands the orchestra; perhaps the orchestra does not understand her") and acknowledged how difficult it was for women to succeed in the field of composition (Marion Bauer: "I know that she has had a terrific struggle and very little opportunity to work out the ideas she has, which demand freedom from worry and plenty of time"). It is also conspicuous that several suggested that she was psychologically unsound in some way (Alvin Johnson: "Both Miss Beyer and her project are a little mad"), or to be avoided at all costs (Mrs. David Mannes: "We wish to emphatically state that we would not think of endorsing the operatic plans Miss Beyer has submitted"). It is unclear why Johnson and Mrs. Mannes were so vehemently negative, given that some prominent people offered more moderate or even overtly supportive views of Beyer's promise as a composer. Though critical of her ability, Copland generously—though perhaps also unhelpfully—pointed out that she was an "honest soul with serious musical pretensions." Cowell himself provided the most profound conclusion of them all—"her whimsy and originality really amount to genius"—even though, in the end, he recommended a male contemporary over Beyer.

Status Quo is lost to us and apparently became lost to Beyer after her Guggenheim proposal was rejected.[11] We can only imagine, based on a few fragments of her global, meta-musical vision, what this work might have become, had it been supported.

10 Beyer's Final Years, 1940–44

THE SUMMER OF 1940, which coincided with Cowell's release from prison, was busy for Beyer. She continued working on Cowell's behalf and also visited him in White Plains after he had settled at the Graingers' house.[1] She taught piano at a number of schools and private homes around the greater New York area, and the families for whom she taught were central to her social life. She spent much of July in Grant City, Staten Island, house-sitting for the family of her gifted ten-year-old piano student Roland Leitner, with whom she was particularly close and to whom she dedicated one of her last works, the Sonatina in C, in 1943. While his family was away she watered their plants, raked leaves, and took care of Roland's pets.[2] That July, for her birthday, Roland gave Beyer $10 and a poem he had written himself; he was particularly eager for her to join the family on their vacation to the Catskills. She would sometimes spend the night at their house after Roland and his brother's piano lessons. (Around this time she also was close to a family for whom she taught piano lessons in Harrington Park, New Jersey, where she also occasionally spent the night after lessons.) After house-sitting for the Leitners, she spent much of August with friends, who seem to have been parents of a young piano student of Beyer's named Herbert, in the seaside town of West Belmar, New Jersey. Beyer, who frequently wrote in her letters about how much she loved to swim, reported to Cowell that "the ocean baths have strengthened me and made me hungry . . . I eat about 10 times as much as I used to!"[3] During the months while Beyer was away, Cowell occasionally visited New York on business and stayed at her apartment, which they apparently considered a shared office space.

After returning from her holiday at the seaside, Beyer's thoughts returned to Cowell and their relationship. From a Hudson River pier near her Jane Street apartment, on August 24, 1940, Beyer wrote Cowell an emotional and revealing letter that freely mixed personal issues with compositional ones:

> Perhaps it will be better to be absolutely frank with you in the case of my friends and relatives . . . Now they have all expected that you will marry me as soon as you are able. Having said that you are not the marrying kind, they concluded that you are a homo-sexual. . . . One day [Beyer's friend; name unclear] surprised me by stating: "Henry and his friends want to get rid of you, mark my word, and when they are ready for it, they will offer you something for the work you have done." I said: "Ausgeschlossen" [out of the question], and if they would, I would certainly not accept it, not a penny! . . . After telling you all this, you might not care to meet any of the bunch, I couldn't blame you. [Beyer's friends: Rie and Herbert Chandière?] said one day, before you were free, about marriage. I answered: Who wants to marry an old sick woman? They said, you are neither old nor sick, in decent circumstances you will soon be alright again, such devotion of yours counts. . . .
>
> It is still strangely exciting to meet you and to find over and over again how much we have in common! I am not entirely free yet and myself at these meetings, I don't know what I may be allowed to do and what not! May friends touch each other?

Though only partially excerpted here, this particular letter, while typical in its tone, is remarkable in several respects. Beyer had admitted her feelings for Cowell quite openly years before, yet her uncertainty about his affection lingered. This letter suggests how charmed she still was by Cowell, to what degree she might have been under pressure from family and friends to marry the man to whom she had been so devoted. It also suggests that her friends saw her more clearly than Cowell did. Yet it is uncertain how much of her belief in their relationship was based on a shared reality. It is equally unclear whether Cowell had at one time truthfully encouraged Beyer to believe in a mutual romantic attachment, or whether he was exploiting her devotion, using her for his own professional survival during his prison years. It is clear, however, that he did not feel obligated to help promote her music, neither in her last years, nor after her death.

From the moment he was released in the summer of 1940 Cowell began distancing himself from Beyer. These efforts might have been intensified due to pressure from his stepmother, Olive, who had never felt that Beyer could be considered a suitable match for Cowell. His attempts to sever his connections to

Beyer might also have increased because he began to envision a partnership with Sidney Robertson, ethnographer and supervisor of the California Folk Music Project, with whom he had developed a deeper friendship during his prison years. Later, Robertson indirectly degraded the work Beyer did for Cowell by describing him (and Robertson's own working relationship with him) in this way: "People say, '[Sidney,] you have always done so much for Henry, [but] I have never really believed this, because I never felt that Henry was a person for whom one could do very much." Perhaps with Beyer in mind, Robertson added: "Practical work, yes, typing letters, yes, running around doing errands yes, but he had a kind of force in himself."[4]

By fall 1940, Cowell actively sought out eligible women for possible marriage.[5] Around this time he included Beyer in a list of composers in a *Modern Music* article titled "Drums Along the Pacific," but he cryptically referred to her as "J. M. Beyer, formerly of New York," to which she responded bewilderedly, "Does it mean now of Staten Island, Harrington Park, and Brooklyn?"[6] Despite his growing indifference, she continued to write about work she was doing for him—negotiating performances with a long list of prominent conductors, recordings, and lecture opportunities. Between summer and fall 1940, Cowell seems to have dismissed any intention of helping Beyer make her work known; instead, he passed on performance and recording opportunities to John Cage, Lou Harrison, and William Russell. At the end of the year he complained to his parents and expressed anguish about his attempts to sever the ties:

> I have been having trouble in my relationship with Hanna Beyer. I had to tell her bluntly that I would never be in love with her. . . . It is very hard to withdraw from her smoothly and slowly, which I have been trying to do, as I sense that there is no future to this relationship (she cannot be a friend) and so it may have to come to an open and definite break. I don't wish this, and am still trying to avoid it.[7]

The Beyer-Cowell correspondence reveals a vast gulf between how each of them viewed the nature of their relationship. Beyer continued to inform Cowell about day-to-day occurrences, disregarding his desire to "withdraw smoothly and slowly." Perhaps his attempt was too slow for her to really take notice. On September 28, 1940, Beyer announced to Cowell that she had received a summons from the director of music at the Board of Education: "Kindly report to the Principal of P.S. 156, Brooklyn, Mr. Israel Goldfarb, Sutter Ave. and Crafton Str., regarding the establishment of an after-school piano class." (A day later, Reynolds noted: "Johanna took course and is eligible for piano teaching in public schools.") On October 15 Beyer wrote to Cowell: "I've just landed the loveliest job!" In

December, she invited him for Christmas goose at her niece's house, apparently still in denial about his intention to end the friendship.

In early January 1941 Cowell visited Beyer at her home and proposed an arrangement in which he would pay her for work she had done for him in the past, so as to eliminate a situation in which he owed her something. Beyer was opposed to the idea, and after his visit she wrote a contradictory letter that mixed deep feelings with level-headedness, personal and compositional details, and a touching kind of optimism regarding the future of both her music and their relationship: "I wanted to close up a certain chapter, but before daring so, I wanted to make sure, that nothing was left undone, and that even the smallest item was clear between us." She added:

> I wrote a movement for winds this afternoon before you came and I was naturally very happy about the [Hans] Kindler letter for both of us. And it seems to me, for me the worst is over: the thought that nobody will ever play my works. I wanted to show you my four movements for strings today, and I have been planning all sorts of works in my mind which I intent [*sic*] to work on this summer.[8]

In early 1941 conductor of the National Symphony Orchestra Hans Kindler had indicated that he was interested in performing Beyer's Symphonic Movement I (1939) and a work of Cowell's, but the performances never took place.[9] A few days later, she wrote to Cowell:

> I shall give you a few facts today. The dissonant note on which you closed our last experience calls forth these facts: I am sick in bed, bleeding. My condition is worse than we both have been wanting to believe. I have been trying frantically to keep out of the hospital. The city would not help me, because they accuse me of having worked for you while I should have stayed in bed and taken care of my health.[10]

Beyer's illness, which became acute in 1941, is difficult to address from such a historical distance. According to Bertha Reynolds, Beyer received a diagnosis of multiple sclerosis in June of that year, and Reynolds later believed that to be the cause of her death.[11] But according to Beyer's death certificate, she had received a diagnosis of amyotrophic lateral sclerosis as early as 1938. In 1936 Beyer mentioned to Cowell that she had had cancer; two years earlier, Reynolds noted in her diary that Beyer was being treated for varicose veins. Lacking medical records, we can only speculate about whether these different diagnoses were accurate, let alone related, and about what caused her to suffer so much physical pain and deterioration during her final three years. Her letters, and Reynolds's diary, however, clearly document a severe affliction that eventually prevented her from taking care of herself.

In the letter excerpted above, though, Beyer moved beyond her physical condition and went on to describe the circumstances of several job offers, one of which required her to play the piano extensively, which she was incapable of doing, since she had been copying parts for Cowell for months instead of practicing. (It is likely that her difficulty in playing the piano at this time also was related to the onset of more serious symptoms stemming from her disease.) She then turned again to her feelings for him, claiming that her "love is not the possessive kind." Taking on an increasingly bitter tone, she added: "It is so fortunate that just at this lowest point things begin to happen with my works. It seems to be God's help, he might believe in my work as composer, as human being, as do the friends who know me. I should think that you would be happy too to think that somebody worthwhile had come into your life."[12] (Around this time, Beyer also bizarrely told Cowell that, as a child, she had foreseen in a dream the details of the two world wars.) During the following weeks she continued to implore him to escort her to various events (a screening of the Disney film *Fantasia*; a Martha Graham performance; various recitals).[13] She learned that her recording of Cowell's *Tocanta* was being abandoned.

A few weeks later, Cowell wrote Beyer a letter that emphatically reemphasized his proposed business arrangement, one in which his prior method of "taking care of the office overhead [was] to discontinue"—including her Jane Street telephone.[14] He suggested two ways of streamlining their professional contact. First, he would pay her union rates for the copying she had done of his compositions (*Tocanta*, *Anthropos*, others) and thereby would carry no further financial obligation to her. Second, he suggested that they split all fees for any lectures, performances, or recordings that resulted directly from her activity. In a detached yet reasonable manner, he expressed concern about her financial situation. Upon his insistence, on February 9, Beyer reluctantly sent Cowell a "bill" listing the scores she had copied for him: 145 pages at the union rate of forty cents a page. Cowell's financial records show that he sent her a check for $12.50 in January 1941—half the fee for a lecture she arranged for him at Columbia University—and another check for $58 in February, for music copying.[15]

In the same letter, he addressed the lingering emotional situation between them: "I am not in love with you, and cannot feel that a marriage between us would prove a happy one." He explained that he wanted to limit his social contact with Beyer, since he wished to meet eligible women at parties and concerts, and felt that Beyer would jeopardize his reputation if he were to be seen with her in public. He announced that he would no longer come to her apartment, "since I can no longer consider it as my place of business as well as yours." He insisted, "I would do anything I could to avoid hurting you, but there is no use avoiding the truth, and I am deeply sorry that the truth is painful." On January 15, the same day Beyer received this letter, her increasingly existential desperation hit a new low:

> May I beg you today, to reconsider our friendship. To forget, what has happened so far, and begin anew, entirely anew. There is a fierce fight within me and it threatens to wreck my body and mind completely. I am too weak to be able to check it. Bertha is worried about me, she asked me, would I go to a hospital if she finds one for me, that was last weekend. Since then, things have grown worse again. I told Bertha that I would fight desperately to be able to hold through till summer when pupils stop anyway, that, if I stop now, I will loose [*sic*] my chance to ever make a living again. Henry, please don't be hard now, when I am so weakened.[16]

A few weeks later Cowell wrote to Robertson about his fifty-percent arrangement with Beyer. He downplayed—or failed to notice—Beyer's emotional appeals: "Hanna has been writing me, but the tone of the letters is a great deal more sensible, and I think it may come thru with no entire unfriendly break." But he added: "I am fully prepared to break entirely if this half and half won't work."[17]

Despite Cowell's threats to abandon their friendship completely, Beyer continued to demonstrate compassion toward him: "Sorry you have to work so hard," she wrote, "[I] wish we had a society where a man with your qualities were provided for so he could serve his art, and so with continuity" (at the same time she admitted "I seem to be sinking lower each week, am in bad shape . . . but I managed to finish the score for Stokowski").[18] Just a few days before Cowell had announced to Roberston his willingness to "break entirely," on January 21, 1941, Beyer said that she was going to stay with her current doctor until "about June" and then would submit herself to a thorough examination and "perhaps to hospital." In the same letter, Beyer described her "boundless" happiness at seeing a Martha Graham performance of the recent works *El Penitente* and *Letter to the World*, a performance at which she would have seen the young Merce Cunningham dance (it is unclear if Cowell attended the recital with her, or just provided tickets).[19] A day later, Bertha Reynolds intervened on Beyer's behalf, with a letter to Cowell:

> The fact that it is my profession to listen to people in trouble and to keep confidences has resulted in my knowing more about [Johanna's] affairs than anyone else probably. . . . I have been worried about her health and yet she is undoubtedly right that to stop now for hospital care would probably destroy the slender chance she has of building up a living in teaching. Undoubtedly she has less than she needs in food and warmth and rest from heavy physical work. At one time I was able to help her but am now able to earn only enough to meet my own obligations. I am afraid it would be difficult for her to get back on Home Relief because of her resistance to answering some of their questions about the work she was

doing for you at the time she dropped out. She has, therefore, no security as far as I can see, except the chance she may have of earning. I hope that you will do all you can to put opportunities in her way, and we must all desire earnestly that she may recover her health.[20]

In March, Beyer seemed resigned to her situation, telling Cowell "there is not much hope for me, unless I give in, and rest completely and then it will be a slow recovery, having waited so long to do something about it: I must undergo an examination." She realized she could no longer play a role in Cowell's life: "Therefore we have to face the facts and I must give up work for you."[21] A week earlier, she told Cowell that a piece of hers had been rejected by a WPA concert review board.[22]

At this time Beyer's work still included both private students and group after-school piano lessons, as she tried to continue working until the summer despite her illness. On April 3, 1941, she outlined her weekly schedule for Cowell:

Tuesday: Harrington Park 1–9 (I may go sometimes earlier in spring)
Wednesday: Brooklyn 2–6 (I also leave earlier on sunny days and sit over there on the shore road in the sun)
Thursday home (sitting in the sun on Ablingdon Square around noon)
Friday: Staten Island leaving at eleven in the morning.
Mondays I am also definitely home till 6.

As her illness rapidly progressed, she described the details to Cowell, who no doubt would rather not have heard them: her increasing inability to leave her apartment except for her teaching duties, her frequent inability to eat or to rise from her bed, and her lack of strength to work on her music. She described the condition graphically, and metaphorically: "My leg has become thinner and shorter steadily, something radical has to be done. But what worries me more is the piercing pains through my heart (caused by our friendship). These pains seem to pierce right through to the spine and cause paralyzing of both legs at times."[23] The deterioration of her leg made it difficult for her to climb her Jane Street apartment stairs, and her neighbors began to help her by bringing up her mail, for example. She wrote: "You see, they were used to my 'dancing' up and down and now I have to pull myself up with my arms and rest in between. I never see them watching me, but they hear me." She assured him: "All this sounds bad and I shall not speak of it again. Perhaps the sun, the rest, and the double amount of pills will help."[24]

Cowell's 1941 datebook contains a few brief references to Beyer. The first is her name at the end of a "to-do" list, on Monday, March 10. The other is written on March 24: "45 cents to Hanna."[25] In June 1941 he told Beyer that he believed "that it is best for us to discontinue contact altogether."[26] He announced he would return her "Indian record" (about which she had reminded him on many occasions) and her copy of *Maestoso*. The destruction of ties was almost complete.

One day after Cowell made his final "break," Beyer's bitterness about his indifference toward her music erupted in an uncharacteristically angry letter, one that alluded to specific situations about which we have no further information:

> Aggravations:
>
> When I visited you in White Plains you showed me a letter by you to the League of Composers, in which you recommended new composers to be played. In vain did I look for my name—I did not say one word. You went to Yaddo, Rochester, WPA, Mahler—I had also works in all these places—you never mentioned anything, I took it silent. There was a possibility with Sevitzky. Did it ever occur to you to say a word for me? You may have, I don't know, you never mentioned anything. When I asked you about the American Music Festival, in a strange way you said, no, you did not know anything about it, but it wasn't a good festival because Riegger was not on. That same evening Richard told me, that it was through your recommendation that he was being played at the festival, that he was not even a member of the League. . . . Then there was that New Music and also recording business. Once you made a lot of fun about the lovely song I had written and that you would see to be one of the jury and that I would win the prize because nobody else could write such a song. Well, not so long ago you had the chance to make that come true, unfortunately somebody informed me about it too late. Once you wrote about the originality, the bare beauty, humor, wit, and what not in my new things, but when you presented me at the New School, I was rather stunned by your remarks but instead of responding (not to speak of aggravation) to your attitude, I tried to master the whole situation and to quiet down the commotion in the audience. It was not only that one woman. Different people in the audience spoke to me afterwards and Schillinger gave me some sound advice. . . . There was the big chance for me with Stokowski. I wrote the work with enthusiasm and dedicated it to him. It is on the score: To Leopold Stokowski and already in this version [at] the Philadelphia library. The work has not been sent back nor have I heard a word and you tell me today casually, it is put aside till next year. That would mean, I cannot do anything with it until then. I really must have advice about it; please: where can I reach Stokowski directly? Or will you ask him what I should do with that work? I surely have made a fool of myself with Mahler through his Stokowski affair of which I wrote you in detail. As you remember, he said he could play my work after the middle of June. However, so far, he has not asked for parts. He has here 3 works of mine: Symphonic Movements I and II and Symphonic opus 5. I am sure that if you expressed interest directly to Mahler now, I might get a chance there. Above all, I ought to hear at least one work once. With all these festivals and goings on and I belonging to two composers organizations since years etc. etc. and having written over 100 works anyway, 6 symphonic works and no chance to hear one of them! Tell them some of my forefathers fought in the Civil War of America, some are English [men?], and that I have alive native

close Irish-English relatives walking around in Washington today. My own father lived for a number of years in France and England, his [moving?] back to Germany was merely accidental! Why do I mention this now? Perhaps because you brought out the 100 % American once too often. All these percentages make me laugh![27]

This remarkable letter shows Beyer finally allowing herself to feel exploited and betrayed by Cowell: for his lack of advocacy, his silence about possible opportunities, his promotion of male colleagues, his chauvinism about her immigrant status. She also clearly felt frustration about having done all the right things—helping others, joining composers' organizations, writing large amounts of music—and having been met with nothing but indifference. Whereas her energy usually emerged as enthusiasm and curiosity, here we witness a justifiably deep anger full of "aggravations" about a kind of unspoken exclusion, one Cowell could have altered easily by being an advocate rather than a gatekeeper.

The last available dated correspondence from Beyer to Cowell, written on June 8, 1941, is a postcard about a check from the Kansas City Philharmonic Orchestra. The immediacy of Beyer's developing illness might have been a convenient way for Cowell to back away from her completely. On June 1, 1940, Reynolds took Beyer to Bellevue Hospital for an exam. (The following day, Lou Gehrig died, after his own battle with ALS.) On June 9, Reynolds wrote: "Johanna told must have operation on her semi-paralyzed leg. No income. I wrote soc. service at Bellevue about her." Less than a month later, Cowell's civil rights were restored, and in September he and Robertson married. It is uncertain whether Cowell and Beyer had any contact after that point. Robertson later claimed that due to Cowell's rejection, Beyer "had some sort of a breakdown, following which she killed herself."[28]

In the absence of further letters to Cowell after summer 1941, or any other evidence aside from Beyer's last dated compositions, we turn again to Bertha Reynolds, who continued to document the painful reality of Beyer's final years. The following are her remaining diary entries mentioning "Johanna," from September 1941 through January 1944:

22 September 1941: Johanna in Bellevue. No diag. yet.

28 September 1941: Visited Johanna at Bellevue. Being seen by big neurologist.

22 October 1941: Visited Johanna. Had injections of Vit. E.—nerve pain and soreness.

1 December 1941: Visited Johanna and taught her solitaire. Out on porch only mornings when sun out. Has multiple sclerosis.

4 January 1942: Erdix for visit over Sun. before going back to army in 2 weeks. Doing churches today and I meet him to go to Bellevue to see Johanna.

9 February 1942: Johanna has invitation to home of a teacher to whom she gave music

lessons. Home Relief will pay board. Bellevue s.w. [social work] hadn't been able to find any place.

16 July 1942: Called on Johanna, now moved to 1st floor apart. her colored helper made the agency find.

23 August 1942: Called on Johanna. John Cage, young composer there.[29]

13 June 1943: Johanna in bad shape. Music Foundation pays for woman to stay with her all day. She is on list for House of the Holy Comforter. Is directing packing and giving away her things. Wanted to give me her terra cotta butter dish since I am the only one of her friends who doesn't have ice. Sec. of Musician's Alliance (?) picked up all her compositions to be cataloged—over 100.[30]

4 July 1943: Johanna went to House of Holy Comforter.

1 August 1943: Call on Johanna. Nurses short.

12 December 1943: Johanna in bed now.

11 January 1944: Johanna died yesterday. Had not seen her since Dec. 12.

16 January 1944: Wednesday forenoon went to Js funeral at House of the Holy Comforter. 3 nieces, Gertrude's husband, and several friends there. Service in chapel, and patients sat in wheelchairs.

Conclusion

"May the Future Be Kind to All Composers"

SHORTLY BEFORE MOVING to the House of the Holy Comforter in June 1943, Beyer supervised the packing of her life's work. These boxes of manuscripts rested at the American Music Center in New York for over two decades. Paul Price, a percussion instructor and assistant professor of music at the University of Illinois in Urbana, was among a small number of people who maintained interest in Beyer's work after her death; in 1953 he attempted to gain information about any heirs. He enlisted Vladimir Ussachevsky (then editor of New Music Editions), who, after consulting with Cowell, provided no information.[1] In 1961 Price conducted a performance of Beyer's March for percussion ensemble at the Manhattan School of Music.[2] Rosario Mazzeo continued to program her Three Songs for Soprano and Clarinet with his Crown Chamber Players between 1966 and 1976. Around 1969 John Cage seems to have considered including an excerpt from one of Beyer's percussion works in his book *Notations*.[3]

In summer 1965 a young Charles Amirkhanian explored the holdings of the American Music Center, and discovered Beyer's "iconoclastic scores . . . languishing in obscurity."[4] A few years later, Peter Garland published the score of *Music of the Spheres*, without commentary, in *Soundings* 7–8 (1973), and Beyer's Three Movements for Percussion appeared in *Soundings* 10 (1976). Subsequently, a number of composers and musicians, including Garland, Michael Byron, Gordon Mumma, Thomas Siwe, and Larry Polansky, began to express curiosity about this mysterious, pioneering figure. In August 1977 *Music of the Spheres* and Three Movements for Percussion were performed at the Cabrillo Music Festival (Santa Cruz, California) on a program called "Only the Lonely: Music of the Experimental Tradition." *Music of the Spheres* was recorded by the Electric Weasel Ensemble and released as the opening track on the "first compilation disc of electronic music by women composers" called *New Music for Electronic and Recorded Media, Women in Electronic Music.*[5] Beyer might have been surprised to find herself in the company of Laurie Anderson, Annea Lockwood, and Pauline Oliveros.

Amirkhanian and New York Public Library librarian Karen Famera tried to track down information about Beyer's life, to no avail: the American Music Center had no biographical records, and the Library of Congress held no records of deposit from her in the copyright office. According to George Boziwick, longtime curator of American Music and chief of the Music Division at the New York Public Library, Beyer's manuscripts remained at the American Music Center until March of 1981, "when they were brought to the New York Public Library as part of a long-standing agreement to transfer scores from the AMC to the NYPL 25 years (or more) after the death of their composer/members."[6] Between 1980 and 1984 clarinetist William Powell at California State University-Long Beach made several attempts to acquire copies of Beyer's clarinet works, writing, "I am very interested in the prospect of bringing to light the works of this much neglected American pioneer."[7]

Not until 1988 did Beyer receive a concert devoted solely to her work. In celebration of the one-hundredth anniversary of her birth, John Kennedy, Charles Wood and the ensemble Essential Music produced two landmark concerts in November at the Greenwich House Music School on Barrow Street in New York. (Kennedy had initially stumbled upon some of Beyer's manuscripts while researching the John J. Becker collection in the Americana Collection at the New York Public Library and was encouraged by Nicolas Slonimsky, who agreed that Beyer "certainly deserves a remembrance."[8]) Kyle Gann wrote a statement for the event: "Almost forgotten now, Johanna Magdalena Beyer was the only woman involved in electronic music in 1930s New York. She worked with Henry Cowell, and experimented with tempo modulation, rhythmic processes, and new electronic instruments as early as or before male counterparts like John Cage."[9] For this occasion Kennedy wrote his essay "'Total Eclipse': The Life of Johanna Magdalena Beyer," based on the small amounts of information available at the time. Making a few understandable but speculative leaps due to a lack of counterevidence, and based on the murky remembrances of John Cage, Sidney Robertson Cowell, Lou

Harrison, William Russell, and Otto Luening, Kennedy wrote that Beyer was "painfully shy" and close to no one, and that she did not maintain ties to family in Germany. Similarly, Amirkhanian's essay—titled "Johanna Magdalena Beyer: A Discovery Waiting to Happen"—reinforced assumptions that Beyer was "socially awkward," "unprepossessing," possibly suffering from "terminal alcoholism," and that she had a "depressing personal existence," a "lack of personal charisma," and "an apparently lonely existence." As we have seen, Beyer was poor and suffered physically and emotionally, but she was neither lonely nor alone.

The charge of *neglect* also loomed large in discussions of Beyer's reception. Reviewing one of the Essential Music concerts, John Rockwell wrote in the *New York Times*: "Johanna Magdalena Beyer was a neglected member of the New York classical-music avant-garde in the 1930's—so neglected that she doesn't even appear in the *New Grove Dictionary of American Music*."[10] He continued: "To judge from Thursday's short program, Miss Beyer was something of an avant-garde dogmatist, determined to work out earnest, radical compositional ideas without much concern for just how the music might sound." Still, very little accurate information was available about Beyer, and scholarly publications, as if trapped in an eternal game of "telephone," continued to repeat and embellish the few fragments that had been written about her. In 1993, for a example, a massive encyclopedic bio-bibliography on women in music erroneously claimed that Beyer was an "opera composer, electronic music composer, [and] musicologist."[11]

Around this time, composer Larry Polansky, then a faculty member at the Mills College Center for Contemporary Music and director of the Mills College Contemporary Performance Ensemble, became interested in Beyer via his research on Ruth Crawford Seeger. In 1994 Polansky announced the establishment of the Frog Peak/Johanna Beyer Project, which enlisted volunteer editors—mostly composers themselves—to edit and annotate Beyer manuscripts, which were published (with facsimiles) and distributed in critical editions by Frog Peak Music, the composers' collective co-founded by Polansky and Jody Diamond. The call for editors included these statements:

> Naturally, we are interested in getting Beyer's work out in performable form first, but we are open to other ideas. *We envision this project as a way for the Frog Peak Collective to facilitate composers taking care of another composer's work. The main idea is to make an important composer's work available for the first time.* There will be no royalties involved in the project, it is purely voluntary.[12]

In 1994, *Bees* was published as the first Frog Peak/Johanna Beyer Project edition; in the following two years a consequential flurry of editorial work brought eight more editions to press. In August 1995, Polansky delivered a paper titled "The

Works of Johanna Magdalena Beyer" at a symposium on American women in music at the University of Colorado at Boulder; a year later, Kennedy and Polansky's groundbreaking article—"'Total Eclipse': The Music of Johanna Magdalena Beyer; An Introduction and Preliminary Annotated Checklist"—was published in *Musical Quarterly*. Including a description of each manuscript held in the New York Public Library and the Fleisher Collection, this fifty-nine-page article has remained the single most valuable resource on Beyer for nearly twenty years. Already the first paragraphs of the article point to the main themes of her reception: obscurity, mystery, enigma.

The twenty-one Frog Peak editions of Beyer's music that are currently available have facilitated an increasing number of performances and recordings of Beyer's music that have in turn stimulated performers and scholars to take up the challenge of studying and disseminating this almost-lost body of work.[13] Some of the recent explorers of this terrain include: pianists Sarah Cahill, Rory Cowal, Judy Gordon, and Deborah Richards; conductor John McCaughey and the Astra Chamber Music Society in Melbourne, Australia; musicians Robert Black, Daniel Goode, and Margaret Lancaster; the Todd Meehan and Doug Perkins Duo; the DownTown Ensemble, which mounted performances of Beyer's songs and clarinet suites during their 2004–05 season; musicologist Melissa de Graaf's study of the Composers' Forum-Laboratory events; Marguerite Boland's theoretical analyses; John Spilker's work on dissonant counterpoint; Ron Coulter's performances, recordings, and analyses of heretofore unknown percussion works; and many more. In 1996 the Astra Choir, conducted by John McCaughey, gave two evenings of Beyer's music, including the premieres of three of Beyer's five choral pieces as well as the sixty-year-old song *Have Faith!* When Astra released its two-CD recording of fourteen of Beyer's compositions in 2008, Art Lange wrote: "The New World release of previously unknown music by Johanna Beyer (under the title 'Sticky Melodies') provided ample evidence of her shamefully *neglected* importance among the American Modernist composers of the 1930s."[14] Preparing for the recording, Astra curated a concert at the Gasworks Theatre in Melbourne on November 4, 2007, that included four of Beyer's five WPA-era choral works. Some of the other pieces on the program had not been heard for some seventy years, following single performances.

Both Beyer the woman and Beyer the composer have been received and interpreted in a variety of ways that warrant further exploration and consideration. Her biography itself is intriguing, and her compositions are important works of their time, but the story of her absence from history following her death is fascinating in and of itself, as is the revival and reassessment of her work in recent decades. From her disappearance from the historical record to the many archival sources, editions, performances, recordings, and works of scholarship that we have available today, Beyer seems to have finally achieved the attention she so desperately—and futilely—sought for her music during her lifetime. In the end we are left with both a paucity of information and a wealth of riches from Beyer's life: a volume of personal and professional correspondence, a diary written by a friend, a few legal documents, a census with misinformation, three photographs, a name spelled wrong on a gravestone—and some fifty-six compositions that deserve to be heard.

APPENDIX A: BIOGRAPHICAL DATA

Annotated Chronology of Selected Events in Johanna Beyer's Life:

July 11, 1888: born in Leipzig, to Bernhard Hermann Beyer (b. 1843–d.?) and Maria Richter Beyer (b. 1850-d. circa 1936). At the time, Leipzig's state of Saxony had recently been absorbed by the newly unified, Prussian-governed German Empire.

September 1, 1905–November 11, 1905: lives at Könneritzstraße 48, Leipzig.

November 11, 1905–March 7, 1909: lives at Könneritzstraße 70, Leipzig.

March 7, 1909: travels (or moves) to Elgershausen, then to Gießen.

Before World War I: citizens' registry papers held at the Leipzig city archive that document Beyer's moves between 1905 and 1911 describe her as a "correspondent, teacher, and music student."[1]

April 24, 1911: arrives at Ellis Island on the *S.S. Washington* from port of Bremen. According to the passenger ship manifest, Beyer paid for her own second-class passage and carried at least \$50. As her destination she lists an uncle Henry Birch, who lives at 661 Columbus Avenue (New York City).[2]

June 21, 1914: returns to Leipzig following her first three-year trip to New York.

From June 27, 1914: lives at her brother-in-law Kühnel's address at Hospitalstraße 26.

March 1, 1915: lives in a household named Michaelis.

March 11, 1915: registers her residence as her parents' house.

April 26, 1915: travels to Dessau.

September 1923: graduates from a German music conservatory (according to Beyer's 1937 curriculum vitae).

November 1923: sails back to the United States on the *S.S. Munich* from Bremen, naming Essen as her last residence. Again she pays for her own passage and is carrying \$25. (Her records also claim that she had never before been to the United States.) She listed her "nearest relative or friend" back home as her mother, in the Leipzig district of Schleußig (Oeserstraße 5). As her final destination she indicates a "friend" named Miss Marie Brueck, at 77 South Munn Street in East Orange, New Jersey.[3]

At the time of her immigration, Beyer is five-foot-six, has brown hair and brown eyes, and, according to the ship-manifest questionnaire, she is neither a polygamist nor an anarchist.

June 1, 1925: New York State Census documents a "Johanna Beyer" at 9 King Street in New Castle, Westchester County, New York, in a household belonging to a wealthy family named Guinzburg. The head of household is listed as Ralph K. Guinzburg, director of the I. B. Kleinert Rubber Company. The family includes Guinzburg's wife, Edna, and three children under age ten. Beyer is listed as "servant" and "governess." Two other German servants work as "butler" and "laundress." A young American man is listed as a chauffeur. The census record states that Beyer is thirty-five years old (in fact, on that date she would have been thirty-six). The entry records that she has been in the country for fourteen years, which would place her entry in 1911, the year Beyer first came to the United States. Ralph Guinzburg held a U.S. patent for an improvement to the garter belt, and in 1925 he co-founded Viking Press with George S. Oppenheim. In January 1938, Beyer includes her former employers, now living at 1165 Park Avenue, on a mailing list for New Music Quarterly Recordings.

May 1927: earns a "diploma for solfege" at the Mannes School of Music.

Circa summer 1927: moves to Sunnyside Gardens, 3961 Forty-Third Street, Long Island City, N.Y.

October 30, 1927: meets Bertha Reynolds, who rents a room in Beyer's Sunnyside home.

May 1928: earns a teacher's certificate at the Mannes School of Music.

August 1928: visits Washington, D.C., with niece Frida Kastner.

January 24, 1930: naturalized as an American citizen.

April 11, 1930: obtains an American passport.

July 5, 1930: travels to Germany.

September 7, 1930: arrives back in New York on the *S.S. Stuttgart* from Bremen.

1931: composes first known dated work (Waltz, for piano).

February 1932: meets Ruth Crawford and Charles Seeger; begins composition lessons.

Summer 1932: submits piece to Olympic Arts Competition.

Circa March 1933: meets Henry Cowell.

October 25, 1933: first known performance of Beyer's work, the Three Songs for Soprano, Piano, and Percussion at the New School for Social Research.

February 12, 1935: earliest extant letter from Beyer to Cowell.

April 17, 1935: obtains a second American passport.

June 5, 1935: travels to Germany; goes from there to London in July for performance of her music; returns to United States in September.

October 1935: Beyer's Sunnyside home forecloses.

May 20, 1936: Beyer's first Composers' Forum-Laboratory concert.

Summer 1936–Summer 1940: extensively involved in Cowell's business affairs while he is incarcerated at San Quentin Federal Penitentiary.

September 1936: moves to 40 Jane Street in Manhattan.

May 19, 1937: Beyer's second Composers' Forum-Laboratory concert.

March 1938: appointed to Promotion Committee for New Music Quarterly Recordings.

1938: diagnosed with amyotrophic lateral sclerosis during this year (according to Beyer's death certificate).

Late 1938: applies for Guggenheim Foundation grant to support work on opera *Status Quo*.

April 9, 1940: census entry for Beyer at 40 Jane Street lists her as "Elsie Beyer" and says that she is thirty-nine years old (she was fifty-two). Her place of birth is given as New York; no college-level education is reported.

Summer 1940: spends much of the summer house-sitting for families of piano students on Staten Island and the New Jersey shore.

January 1941: becomes ill; is told she has multiple sclerosis in June.

Summer 1941: last known correspondence between Beyer and Cowell.

September 1941: enters Bellevue Hospital; is treated for nerve pain by neurologist.

July 1942: moves to 303 West Eleventh Street.

June 1943: oversees the packing of her manuscripts for storage at a musicians' organization; that month she also composes her last dated work.

Early July 1943: moves to House of the Holy Comforter, Bronx.

January 9, 1944: Johanna Beyer dies. A funeral is held at the House of the Holy Comforter one week later. On her death certificate, the cause of death is listed as amyotrophic lateral sclerosis. Beyer's niece Frida notifies the Philadelphia-based Fleisher Collection of her aunt's death.[4]

APPENDIX B: CHRONOLOGICAL LIST OF BEYER'S KNOWN WORKS

1931
Waltz, solo piano

1932
Suite for Clarinet I
Suite for Clarinet Ib

193?
Dissonant Counterpoint, solo piano

1933
Percussion Suite in 3 Movements
Suite for Clarinet and Bassoon
Quintet for Woodwinds
Sky-Pieces, soprano and piano (poem by Carl Sandburg)
Three Songs for Soprano, Percussion, and Piano ("Timber Moon"; "Stars, Songs, Faces"; "Summer Grass"; all poems by Carl Sandburg)

1933–34
String Quartet No. 1

1934
Gebrauchs-Musik, solo piano
Ballad of the Star-Eater, soprano and clarinet
Three Songs for Soprano and Clarinet ("Total Eclipse"; "Universal-Local"; "To Be"; all texts by Beyer)

1934–35
Piano-Book: "Classic-Romantic-Modern"

1935
Percussion, suite in five movements (including "*IV*")
March, large ensemble
The Robin in the Rain, choir

1936
Sonata for B-flat Clarinet and Piano
Suite for Bass Clarinet and Piano
Movement for Double Bass and Piano
Movement for Two Pianos
String Quartet No. 2
Clusters (or, *New York Waltzes*), solo piano
Winter Ade and five other folk song settings, solo piano
The Federal Music Project, choir

1936–37
Have Faith! soprano and flute (text by Beyer)

1937
Suite for Violin and Piano
CYRNAB, chamber orchestra
The Main-Deep, choir
The People, Yes, choir
The Composers Forum-Laboratory, choir
Fragment for Chamber Orchestra
Symphonic Suite

1938
Movement for Woodwinds
Movement for String Quartet ("Dance")
Music of the Spheres, three electrical instruments or strings, from *Status Quo*
Elation, concert band
Reverence, wind ensemble
Dance for Full Orchestra, from *Status Quo*

1939
March for 30 Percussion Instruments
Percussion, opus 14
Three Movements for Percussion
Waltz for Percussion
Six Pieces for Oboe and Piano
Suite for Oboe and Bassoon
Suite for Piano
Symphonic Movement I
Symphonic Opus 3

1940
Symphonic Opus 5

1941
Symphonic Movement II
Strive, percussion ensemble

1942
Horizons, percussion ensemble

1943
Sonatina in C, solo piano

194?
Trio for Woodwinds

1943?
String Quartet No. 4

Undated
Prelude and Fugue (in C Major), solo piano
Bees, solo piano
"Three More Pieces for Oboe and Piano, to Joseph Marx, Cincinnati"

APPENDIX C: PUBLICATIONS OF BEYER'S MUSIC

Individual Publications

IV. Percussion ensemble. New Music Orchestra Series No. 18, New Music Editions (1936).
Music of the Spheres. For three electrical instruments or strings. Facsimile. *Soundings* 7–8 (1973).
Three Movements for Percussion. Percussion ensemble. Facsimile. *Soundings* 10 (1976).
Sonata for Clarinet and Piano. Volker Hemken, ed. Friedrich Hofmeister Musikverlag (2009).
Suite for Bass Clarinet and Piano. Volker Hemken, ed. Friedrich Hofmeister Musikverlag (2009).
Percussion. Percussion ensemble. Edited by Ron Coulter. Smith Publications (2012).

Frog Peak Music/Johanna Beyer Project

Frog Peak editions of Beyer's music include copied and edited scores, editorial notes, and facsimiles of the original manuscripts. Series editor: Larry Polansky.

Bees. Solo piano. Copied and edited by Larry Polansky (1994).
Movement for Double Bass and Piano. Copied and edited by David Fuqua (1995).
Ballad of the Star-Eater. Clarinet and soprano. Copied and edited by Charles Shere (1996).
The Federal Music Project. Chorus. Copied and edited by Margaret Fisher and Lou Harrison (1996).
Dissonant Counterpoint. Solo piano. Copied and edited by David Fuqua (1994).
Three Songs for Soprano and Clarinet. Copied and edited by Mark Warhol (1996).
String Quartet No. 2. Copied and edited by Pamela Marshall (1996).
Gebrauchs-Musik. Solo piano. Copied and edited by Carter Scholz (1996).
Movement for Two Pianos. Copied and edited by Drew Krause (1996).
Suite for Violin and Piano. Copied and edited by Kim Bastin (2004).
March for 30 Percussion Instruments. Copied and edited by J. B. Smith (2004).

Publications of Beyer's Music

Have Faith! Flute and soprano. Copied and edited by William Matthews, with editorial assistance from Margaret Lancaster and Beth Griffiths (2005).
Three Movements for Percussion. Copied and edited by Thomas Smetryns (2005).
Waltz for Percussion. Copied and edited by Thomas Smetryns (2005).
Percussion Opus 14. Copied and edited by Thomas Smetryns (2005).
Suite for Clarinet I. Edited by Daniel Goode, copied by Dennis Bathory-Kitsz (2006).
Suite for Clarinet IB. Copied and edited by Marguerite Boland (2007).
Percussion Suite. Copied and edited by Ron Coulter (2010).
Movement for String Quartet. Copied and edited by Andrew Kohn (2010).
Clusters. Edited by Amy C. Beal, with Dennis Bathory-Kitsz and Larry Polansky (2010).
Suite for Piano. Edited by Amy C. Beal, with Jay Arms (2014).

APPENDIX D: SELECTED RECORDINGS OF BEYER'S MUSIC

A number of important live and archival recordings in private hands or housed in research facilities are not listed here, including recordings made by the John Cage Percussion Players, Westdeutscher Rundfunk, Essential Music, the Astra Chamber Players, Rory Cowal, and the DownTown Ensemble, to name just a few.

1938
Suite for Clarinet and Bassoon; II. *Lentamente* and IV. *Allegro ponderoso*
Rosario Mazzeo, clarinet, and Raymond Allard, bassoon. New Music Quarterly Editions 1413A-B (78 RPM).

1977
Music of the Spheres
Electric Weasel Ensemble with Charles Amirkhanian. *New Music for Electronic and Recorded Media, Women in Electronic Music*. 1750 Arch Street. [Re-released by New World Records in 2006.]

1991
IV
Essential Music. *The Aerial* no. 3. Non Sequitur Recordings.

2001
Gebrauchs-Musik and *Dissonant Counterpoint*
Sarah Cahill, piano. *9 Preludes*. New Albion Records 114.

2003
Suite for Clarinet IB
Patrick O'Keefe, clarinet. Zeitgeist, *If Tigers Were Clouds*. Innova Recordings.

2006
Suite for Violin and Piano
Miwako Abe, violin; Michael Kieran Harvey, piano. *Works for Violin by George Antheil,*

Johanna Beyer, Henry Cowell, Charles Dodge, Ruth Crawford, David Mahler, Larry Polansky, Stefan Wolpe. New World Records 80641-2.

2008

Fourteen chamber, vocal, and choral works

John McCaughey and the Astra Chamber Music Society. *Sticky Melodies*. New World Records 80678-2.

2009

Have Faith!

Margaret Lancaster, flute; Beth Griffith, soprano. *Io*. New World Records 80665-2.

2011

IV; *Percussion Op. 14*; *Three Movements for Percussion*; *Waltz*; *Percussion Suite*

Meehan/Perkins Duo and the Baylor Percussion Group. *Restless, Endless, Tactless: Johanna Beyer and the Birth of American Percussion Music*. New World Records 80711-2.

Movement for Double Bass and Piano

Robert Black, bass; John McDonald, piano. *Modern American Bass*. New World Records 80722-2.

2012

Strive; *Percussion*; *Horizons*

Ron Coulter and the Southern Illinois University Carbondale Percussion Group. *Origins: Forgotten Percussion Works, Vol. 1*. Kreating SounD 4.

APPENDIX E: BEYER'S POETRY

TOTAL ECLIPSE

Moving of masses,
Stirred by astro-phenomena,
Directing matter,
Their slave, yet their master,
Still to be.

Effort, research, action,
Thought bearing power, strength,
And courage abundant
To wrestle from the elements
The secret kept.

The world is aghast,
Nature pales in hush
And feeble protesting
Sinks into last motions,
Activity before death.

Birds and beasts bow in fear,
Frightened leaves tremble,
Emaciated sunbeams die below swaying grass,
Leaving the planet colorless,
Faint, deathlike at rest.

Here and yonder,
Beads of light—lost,
Erring through valleys of the moon,
Still shed their love upon earth,
While shadow-bands pattern designs.

But behold the heavens,
Phenomenous climax!
Bursting the shielding surface,

The fiery glow of the corona
Circles its dance of life.

And its secrets alight,
Reaching out beyond spheres,
Expanding toward searching,
Restless thoughts of men,
Begging to be known, to be loved.

But though men try,
Time and again,
These longing elements flee back,
Hiding their shame—"misunderstood"—
Wearing mourning-veils another time untold!

TO BE

To be a sunbeam, a sparkling ray,
To fall as raindrop, chattering gay,
To be a grain of sand, bathing in sun and wind,
Waiting for tides to come and go—
To be a tiny shoot, just from home "root,"
To leaf off from the stem that holds you firm,
To be a blossom, oh, with spellbound hue,
Forthcoming fruit promise, crystalled in dew—
To be a wandering cloud, sailing along,
To shine as star above, meet moons and sun,
To rise and fall in curves, in space and time,
Thus, an enduring cycle, majestic, sublime.

UNIVERSAL-LOCAL

Stars, moons, suns,
Penetrating love—
Endless time, infinite space—
Forever—
Boundless beauty—

Sleepers, toiling with a minute,
With a grain of soil—
Poor, forgotten creatures, dragging on—
But void,
Where could be wings!

HAVE FAITH!

Here is a song for you,
oh, nightingale!
a song of what!
of hope, of future, present, past?
it does not matter, it does not matter.
But essential is,
that you and I and all the others
have faith in things to come,
in things that passed, and are
and we must try to understand
and love and help each other,
have faith in things to come,
have faith!

THE FEDERAL MUSIC PROJECT

I know of an active bee-hive,
it busses [buzzes] and bubles [*sic*] all day,
is full of creative ideas,
a nucleus of a future so gay!

To it come all happy children
and adults so young and so old
to find the key to music,
to know of the secrets untold.

It all is taught with knowledge
with love through games and fun.
Unavoidably what may happen
is surely a wonderful thing.

Glad people will breath [*sic*] in music,
the babies with their milk
and soon we will have creators
of enduring music and skill.

The Federal Music Project,
the bee-hive I'm talking about,
is a remarkable living idea
with a future, oh, so bright!

THE COMPOSERS FORUM-LABORATORY

If you are a composer,
and don't know what to do,
go to the Forum-Laboratory
they'll surely hear you.
Whether "old" or "new,"
abstract or true,
quite fancy or plain,
for orchestra or choir,
percussion or piano,
woodwinds or strings,
a Mass or a dance,
they'll give you your chance,
and furnish an audience, so big as the hall,
who comes to see, to hear, to know,
whether it is really so
that we have composers, quite a long row,
who will bear testimony of our epoch
so great, so tense,
so vast, so immense,
full of vigor and strength,
fateful at glance
but of future enhanced
and response we get spontaneously
just you are being criticized on the spot
whether you like it or not,
and all is recorded,
so you better be for it,
The Composers Forum-Laboratory.

NOTES

Introduction

1. See Appendix A for a selected and annotated chronology of Beyer's known addresses, travels, and key life events.

2. Beyer's 1937 CV accompanied her 1938 Guggenheim application. This important document is held in both the Serge Koussevitzky Collection and the Nicolas Slonimsky Collection in the Music Division, Library of Congress.

3. It is unclear when and where Beyer might have studied with Rudhyar. In an undated letter to Cowell (probably 1941), Beyer expressed doubt about listing Rudhyar as one of her teachers on official documents.

4. Amyotrophic lateral sclerosis, or ALS, is also known as "Lou Gehrig's disease," after the legendary New York Yankee who died of ALS on June 2, 1941, the day after Beyer was examined at Bellevue Hospital for her severely deteriorated condition purportedly caused by advanced ALS.

5. John McCaughey, program notes for Astra 2007, "Johanna Magdalena Beyer, Chamber and Choral Works 1931–36," concert at Gasworks Theatre, Melbourne, November 4, 2007.

6. See, for example, Elizabeth Hinkle-Turner, *Women Composers*, 13, 90.

7. See Spilker, "Origins," 516. According to Spilker's analysis, less than a third of Beyer's works use dissonant counterpoint techniques.

8. Siwe, "Lou Harrison," 30.

9. Composers' Forum Transcripts, May 19, 1937; see de Graaf, "Documenting Music," 91.

10. However, neither Tick nor Hicks had access to Beyer's letters in the Cowell papers at the New York Public Library; that collection was still sealed at the time of these publications.

11. Several manuscripts and copies are held at the Fleisher Collection in the Free Library of Philadelphia, and several percussion ensemble scores are held in the John Cage Papers at Northwestern University.

12. Beyer Scores (1931–1943), JPB 82-77; Kennedy and Polansky, "'Total Eclipse.'"

13. Cowell Papers, JPB 00-03.

14. Reynolds Papers.
15. Woolfe, "Composers," 73.

Chapter 1. Sunnyside

1. Reynolds, *Uncharted Journey*, 105.
2. Reynolds, "Informal Autobiography," typescript, held in the Reynolds Papers.
3. Reynolds, *Uncharted Journey*, 105.
4. I am grateful to Herbert Reynolds of the Sunnyside Gardens Historic District Council for providing this information.
5. Beyer might have been able to save up the average $1,000 to $2,000 down payment for a new home in Sunnyside through her work for the wealthy Guinzburg family around 1925.
6. Stein, *Toward New Towns*, 34.
7. Unless otherwise noted, specific details about Beyer's Sunnyside community and daily life are taken from Bertha Reynolds diaries held in the Reynolds Papers.
8. In December 1931, Reynolds took Beyer and a friend named Dorothy Jenks to the debut concert of the eighteen-year-old piano student of Abby Whiteside's—and later Pulitzer Prize–winning composer—Morton Gould.
9. Quoted in Schwartz, "New Negro Renaissance," 54.
10. Gregory, "Drama of Negro Life," 158.
11. "F. Eugene Corbie Dies at Home in Trinidad," *New York Age*, October 20, 1928.
12. The household was one of politics but also healthy eaters: on February 20, 1929, Reynolds recorded a dinner of brown rice and mushrooms for herself, Beyer, and Beyer's niece Frida; on other occasions, recipes for shared salads are described.
13. For example, on May 23, 1929, Beyer accompanied a singer and a violinist in a musical program for the Mothers' Club of P.S. 125 in Woodside; see "Fathers Invited to Mothers' Meeting," *Daily Star* (Queens Borough), May 22, 1929.
14. Many thanks to Herbert Reynolds for locating these *Sunnyside News* ads in the E. E. Wood Papers.
15. Perhaps due to the economic collapse of the Depression, around 1938 piano teachers at the Greenwich House Music School were still only paid between $1.00 and $2.70 per hour.
16. *Games of the 10th Olympiad.* I have not been able to determine which piece she sent to the competition.
17. See Kennedy and Polansky, "'Total Eclipse,'" 720.

Chapter 2. Compositional Beginnings

1. Bick, "Tradition of Dissent," 141, 181.
2. The enrollment for this course listed just four participants, including Jessie Baetz, a pianist who would later take lessons from and perform with Beyer, and live in the same building at 40 Jane Street around 1940.
3. Siwe, "Lou Harrison," 30.

4. This concert, titled "A Program of American Music," took place on March 12, 1933. The program included music by Marion Bauer, John Becker, Aaron Copland, Henry Cowell, Ruth Crawford, Celius Dougherty, Charles Ives, Wallingford Riegger, and Carl Ruggles.

5. Crawford, *America's Musical Life*, 590.

6. Unless otherwise noted, all quoted letters from Beyer to Cowell, as well as correspondence between Cowell and his parents, Beyer and Cowell's parents, and all of Cowell's prison years (1936–1940) correspondence are held in the Henry Cowell Papers at the New York Public Library.

7. On July 13, 1935, Richard Strauss resigned his post as president of the Reichsmusikkammer. The following month, the Reichsmusikkammer issued a decree forbidding Jews and other non-Aryans from participating in German orchestras. See Slonimsky, *Music Since 1900*, 394.

8. This letter is held in the "programs and clippings" section of the Ruth Crawford Seeger Papers. The letter was written on the back of a program for a concert of "Works by American Women" at the Society of Women Musicians on December 8, 1934. The concert was arranged by Fiona McCleary and Katharine Eggar in conjunction with the New York International Exchange Concerts. The program included music by Marion Bauer, Evelyn Berckmann, Suzanne Bloch, Ethel Glenn Hier, Marguerite Fischel, Fiona McCleary, and Gena Branscombe. A note at the bottom of program announced: "The Council much regrets that owing to difficulties of rehearsal, it has not been possible to include three songs (*Rat Riddles*, *Prayers of Steel*, and *Honeybees*) for Contralto, Oboe, Percussion and Pianoforte by Ruth Crawford."

9. This letter provides evidence that Beyer knew the Seegers reasonably well and considered herself a friend. She used the more intimate signature "Hanna" in letters to Cowell and presumably with other close friends and family. She also alluded to the fact that she knew that another Seeger child was on the way. In fact, Peggy Seeger was born on June 17, 1935, just twelve days after Beyer left for Europe.

10. According to Kennedy and Polansky's description of Beyer's String Quartet No. 2 (1936), the name "Persephone" is crossed out on the front page of the manuscript. Beyer's letters frequently referred to the myths of Persephone and Prometheus, and she often used the phrase "Sunny Hades." Her first three letters to Cowell are all addressed to Sunny Hades. Even after Cowell's arrest she addressed his letters to Sunny Hades (those letters ended up at the Sheriff's office in Redwood City, California) until Alvin Johnson strongly advised her to stop doing so (see letter from Beyer to Olive Cowell, September 19, 1936). Several letters to Olive Cowell were also addressed to Sunny Hades. Sunny Hades also seems to have referred to Beyer's own basement in Sunnyside, where she lived for some time after her foreclosure and before moving to Jane Street.

11. "New York Philharmonic Sponsors Concert," *Musical America*, April 25, 1936.

12. Letter from Beyer to Cowell, postmarked June 4, 1941, Cowell Papers. This letter is examined in greater detail in chapter 10.

13. For an in-depth description and analysis of Beyer's 1936 and 1937 Composers' Forum-Laboratory events, see de Graaf, *Forum Concerts*.

14. "Two Composers Heard."

Chapter 3. Having Faith

1. Beyer's three-story Greek Revival building, built in 1845 as a block of several residential and commercial buildings at the intersection of Jane Street and Eighth Avenue, had greatly deteriorated by the late 1960s, was nearly destroyed by a fire in 1972, and was then demolished. Soon after, the Jane Street Block Association turned the site into a neighborhood garden.

2. Beyer added: "Already I am loved up here at the school"; letter from Beyer to Olive, August 1, 1936, Cowell Papers.

3. Letters from Beyer to Olive during the second half of 1936; letter from Beyer to Alvin Johnson, August 30, 1936, Cowell Papers.

4. Beyer mentioned that Alvin Johnson blamed Cowell's heavy sentence on the "public hysteria over sex-crimes out there" in a letter to Olive, August 30, 1937, Cowell Papers.

5. She wrote "especially since my cancer" to Cowell on June 24, 1936, with no further commentary. I have not found any other evidence of an earlier illness or references to medical conditions prior to 1941 except for this entry in Reynolds's diary on October 3, 1934: "Johanna having varicose veins treated."

6. Beyer announced the completion of her quartet to Cowell in a letter written on June 9, 1936, Cowell Papers.

7. This is probably not the "Indian record" Beyer wrote to Cowell about on June 2, 1941; in an undated letter from around the same time, she mentions a "Shan Kar" [*sic*] record that Cowell had borrowed from her: this was possibly a record titled "The Original Uday Shankar Company of Hindu Musicians, Recorded During the Historic 1937 Visit to the United States," which was originally released in 1938.

8. A biographical sketch for Beyer, possibly intended for the New Music Quarterly Recording of the Suite for Clarinet and Bassoon, lists in her works "one stage play for students: The Modern Composer, lyrics and incidental music" (Cowell Papers).

9. I have speculated about whether Beyer is in the photograph, but given the image in her 1935 passport photo, I do not believe that she is.

10. See letter from Beyer to Olive, April 24, 1937, Cowell Papers.

11. Selections from "The Nature of Melody" have been published in Higgins, *Essential Cowell.*

12. "Concert at WPA Theatre." See also de Graaf, *Forum Concerts.*

13. The photograph in question was located by Melissa J. de Graaf in the Composers' Forum papers at the National Archives and Records Administration and has been reproduced in de Graaf, "'Never Call Us Lady Composers,'" 291; de Graaf, "Intersection," 8; and Beal, "Her Whimsy," 1.

14. Charles Seeger, "Ruth Crawford," in Cowell, *American Composers*, 114.

15. Letter from Cowell to Olive, August 14, 1937, Cowell Papers.

16. Beyer gave Olive the address of Reynolds, 3947 Forty-Eighth Street in Long Island City (announcing, "I still have my New York apartment, I just stay here for the summer months"). She told Koussevitzky that she would be returning to Jane Street on September 16, 1937.

17. Letter from Olive to Beyer, August 24, 1937, Cowell Papers.

18. Letter from Cowell to Beyer, August 15, 1937, Cowell Papers.

19. Thanks to John Kennedy for demystifying the meaning of *CYRNAB*.

20. On November 30, 1937, Reynolds wrote: "J. writing another symphony. Has to pay $100 to have recording made of her comp. by Bst. Symph. Players. (Performances have been very poor and she can never get her works known.)"

21. "Composers Organize," 92–95. Kennedy and Polansky posit that this article may have been written by Aaron Copland himself ("'Total Eclipse,'" 765).

22. Letter from Beyer to Olive Cowell, September 16, 1939, Cowell Papers. Many other letters from this period document Beyer's management of Cowell's financial affairs while he was in prison.

23. This portion of Cowell's prison correspondence is contained in the Cowell Papers.

24. Otto Koischwitz later became a Nazi propagandist during World War II. See chapter 4, note 6.

25. Beyer is not mentioned in George Boziwick's discussion of "materials [in the New York Public Library] that shed light on how Cowell coped with his prison existence." See Boziwick, "Henry Cowell," 51.

26. Letter from Cowell to Blanche Walton, February 1, 1938, Cowell Papers.

27. Letter from Cowell to Harry Cowell, February 1, 1939, Cowell Papers.

28. Letter from Cowell to Becker, March 31, 1940, Cowell Papers. Cowell was acknowledging several radio broadcast performances of his work during March 1940, which Beyer had arranged with Wallenstein, Sevitzsky, and Solomon.

29. See Beyer's "invitation" for the event, reproduced in Kennedy and Polansky, "'Total Eclipse,'" 722.

30. Letter from Beyer to Olive Cowell, February 12, 1940, Cowell Papers.

31. Letter from Beyer to Sevitzky, February 29, 1940, Sevitzky Papers.

32. Letter from Beyer to Sevitzky, April 17, 1941, Sevitzky Papers.

33. See, for example, letters from Beyer to Koussevitzky, Sevitzky, and Alvin Johnson, all written on March 10, 1940; similar letters exists to Quincy Porter, dated March 17, 1940 (Porter Papers) and Lou Harrison, dated March 25, 1940 (Harrison Papers). In a letter to Charles Ives written on May 24, 1940, Beyer announced, "I have over 40 wonderful letters from prominent people all over the States" (Ives Papers); I am grateful to Robin Preiss for transcribing and sharing this letter. Beyer had written the same thing to Sevitzky, April 12, 1940 (Sevitzky Papers).

34. Letter from Beyer to Grainger, March 24, 1940, Grainger Papers. All letters from the Grainger correspondence were made available by Larry Polansky.

35. Letter from Beyer to Sevitzky, May 14, 1940, Sevitzky Papers.

36. On May 16, 1940, Cowell wrote to Grainger: "My parents and Johanna Beyer will be the only ones I shall tell of this plan, and I shall tell them not to inform anyone else"; see also Cowell to Grainger, June 5, 1940, and Cowell to Grainger, June 29, 1940, Cowell Papers.

37. Letter from Cowell to Grainger, June 5, 1940, Cowell Papers.

Chapter 4. New York Waltzes

1. The festival took place on May 7, 1931. In addition to Seeger's lecture, the festival included a program of compositions by Marion Bauer and others.

2. Bauer, *Twentieth-Century Music* (1933), revised edition (1947), 256. Internal quotation marks are Bauer's.

3. See Tick, *Ruth Crawford Seeger*, 22–23; letter from Beyer to Cowell, December 17, 1935, Cowell Papers.

4. Letter from Beyer to Cowell, December 17, 1935, Cowell Papers.

5. See *Bees*, Frog Peak/Johanna Beyer Project No. 1, editorial notes by Larry Polansky.

6. On November 5, 1934, Reynolds wrote in her journal: "Johanna composing a book of rhymes for teaching music to chn. And Dr. Koischwitz to illustrate it." In 1938 Beyer listed Sunnyside resident Professor Otto Koischwitz as a possible future subscriber to New Music Quarterly Recordings. Six illustrations of seasonal scenes signed "O.K." are included in the manuscript of *Piano-Book*. German-born, U.S.-naturalized, Sunnyside resident Oscar Max (Otto) Koischwitz was later accused of treason when he returned to Nazi Germany and worked as a propagandist during World War II. He died of tuberculosis in Berlin in 1944 before he could stand trial.

7. See Kennedy and Polansky, "'Total Eclipse,'" 742.

8. Letter from Cowell to "Father and Mother," March 9, 1938, Cowell Papers.

Chapter 5. Horizons

1. Oteri, "Sounds Heard."

2. Kennedy and Polansky, "'Total Eclipse,'" 726.

3. Kennedy, "Restless—Endless—Tactless," 11.

4. Percussionist and scholar Ron Coulter asserts: "It is worth noting that Beyer's earliest percussion work, Percussion Suite (1933), is only predated by three other percussion works: Amadeo Roldán's *Ritmicas V & VI* (1930), Edgard Varèse's *Ionisation* (1931), and William Russell's *Fugue* (1931–32). The [exact] completion date for *Percussion Suite* is unknown and therefore could possibly also be predated by William Russell's *Three Dance Movements* (April 1933), José Ardévol's *Estudio en forma de preludio y fuga* (May 1930 to June 3, 1933), and/or John J. Becker's *The Abongo: a primitive dance for percussion orchestra with 2 solo dancers & dance group* (1933)." Coulter, "Forgotten Works," 2.

5. Kennedy, "Restless—Endless—Tactless," 11.

6. The complete suite was edited by Coulter and published by Smith Publications in 2012.

7. Coulter, "Forgotten Works," 6, 7.

8. I am grateful to Gordon Mumma for providing documentation of these performances.

9. Kennedy, "Restless—Endless—Tactless," 7.

10. Ibid., 10.

11. Coulter, "Forgotten Works," 8. The Cage *Notations* collection at Northwestern holds Cage's copies of *Strive* and *Horizons*.

12. Ibid., 9.

13. Thanks to Melissa de Graaf for pointing out this connection.

14. Beyer to Harrison, July 11, 1942, Harrison Papers.

Chapter 6. The People, Yes

1. Crawford's *Three Songs to Poems by Carl Sandburg* was published by Cowell in the New Music Orchestra Series in 1933. According to Tick, who cites Charles Amirkhanian, Beyer translated Sandburg poems for the Universal Edition of Crawford's *Three Songs*. A manuscript source in the Ruth Crawford Papers in the Library of Congress names Beyer as the translator for "Prayers of Steel" only, dated November 1932, the same year Beyer met and began studying with the Seegers. (See also Mead, *Henry Cowell's New Music*, 223.)

2. *Sky-Pieces* was performed by Beth Griffith and Michael Blake in Johannesburg, South Africa, on July 3, 2003, in what might have been the world premiere of this song, seventy years after its composition.

3. See Tick, *Ruth Crawford Seeger*, 183.

4. See Rubin, *Songs of Ourselves*, 139–40.

5. See Boland, "Experimentation and Process."

6. Polansky, "Sticky Melodies," 13.

7. Woods's poem was published in 1911 in book called *A Harp of the Heart*; it had been previously published in 1904 in a New York publication called *Current Literature*.

8. A young William Schuman won the contest.

9. *The Main-Deep* was included in Stephens's *A Poetry Recital*, published in June 1925.

Chapter 7. Sonatas, Suites, and String Quartets

1. Katie Clare Mazzeo, personal communication with the author, February 24, 2013. According to Mrs. Mazzeo, this piece was listed as part of the Crown Chamber Players' repertoire during this ten-year span while Rosario Mazzeo was still playing. She added: "He spoke to me several times of his admiration for her writing."

2. Boland, "Experimentation and Process."

3. See Spilker, "Origins," 481–533.

4. Boland, "Experimentation and Process."

5. See Cowell, *New Musical Resources*, 98–108.

6. Polansky has written at length about Beyer's clarinet suites: see Kennedy and Polansky, "'Total Eclipse,'" 752–55; Polansky, "Sticky Melodies," 9–13; and Polansky (with Marguerite Boland), "Tempo Melodies in the Johanna Beyer Clarinet Suites (Fourth Movements)" (2008), available at http://eamusic.dartmouth.edu/~larry/beyerjpegs/beyer_tempo_melodies_boland_polansky.pdf (accessed July 10, 2014).

7. See Kennedy and Polansky, "'Total Eclipse,'" 721; and Siwe, "Lou Harrison," 30.

8. Copland, "Scores and Records," 122–25.

9. Bassist Robert Black gave the world premiere of the Movement for Double Bass and Piano in New York City on December 14, 1995, with Anthony de Mare at the piano.

10. Carl, *Modern American Bass*, 4.

11. See Kennedy and Polansky, "'Total Eclipse,'" 723, 767.

12. Polansky, "Sticky Melodies," 17.

13. Mozart apparently borrowed the melody from a German folksong about religious righteousness; I am grateful to Rachel Lumsden for bringing this to my attention. Lums-

den has speculated about the significance of this quotation and its meaning, in the context of Cowell's imprisonment and Beyer's offer to marry him around the time she wrote the String Quartet No. 2. See Lumsden, "Beyond Modernism's Edge."

14. For a longer analytic description of Beyer's String Quartet No. 2, see Polansky, "Sticky Melodies," 18–20.

Chapter 8. Symphonic Striving

1. In Arthur Cohn's announcement about the Fleisher Collection in *Modern Music*, he included Beyer in the group of "tone-clusterites." See Cohn, "Americans," 116–19.

2. Tick, "Women," 105.

3. In a letter to Koussevitzky written from Sunnyside on August 8, 1937, Beyer announced, "I have just finished my First Symphony, that is, I call it: Symphonic Suite" (Koussevitzky Collection).

4. Letter from Beyer to Grainger, November 15, 1937, Grainger Papers. Some seventeen letters from Beyer to Grainger exist from November 1937 through June 1940.

5. Letter from Beyer to Grainger, April 22, 1939, Grainger Papers.

6. See Kennedy and Polansky for further details on the Beyer-Grainger connection, and for longer excerpts from the Beyer-Grainger correspondence in general.

7. Letter from Cowell to Grainger, May 16, 1939, Cowell Papers.

8. Letter from Beyer to Grainger, May 16, 1939, Grainger Papers.

9. See Kennedy and Polansky, "'Total Eclipse,'" 739.

10. Koussevitzky's comment is included in Beyer's 1938 Guggenheim file. See also letter from Beyer to Olga Naoumoff, Secretary to Koussevitzky, May 16, 1938, Koussevitzky Collection.

11. Beyer to Harrison, July 11, 1942, Harrison Papers.

Chapter 9. Status Quo

1. On August 8, 1937, Beyer wrote to Koussevitzky about her Guggenheim application; on October 11, 1937, she sent him her 1937 CV and "work plan" for *Status Quo* (Koussevitzky Collection).

2. This list is not exhaustive.

3. Letter from Beyer to Koussevitzky, October 11, 1937, Koussevitzky Collection.

4. Beyer, "Work Plan" for Guggenheim Foundation grant proposal, 1937; copies held with Beyer's 1937 CV in the Koussevitzky Collection and the Slonimsky Collection, Library of Congress.

5. Letter from Beyer to Grainger, August 14, 1938, Grainger Papers.

6. Mary Kiffer (Guggenheim Foundation), correspondence with the author, September 12, 2007.

7. Letter from Green to Charles Amirkhanian, March 6, 1977, quoted in Amirkhanian, "Johanna Magdalena Beyer."

8. A copy of this typescript introduction is held in Grainger Papers (Melbourne) and in the Grainger Papers at the Library of Congress.

9. A copy of Beyer's Guggenheim file was obtained from the Guggenheim Foundation.

10. Hannas was the first woman to earn a doctorate in music in the United States, graduating from the Eastman School of Music in 1934.

11. Nonetheless, the 1987 edition of Aaron I. Cohen's *International Encyclopedia of Women Composers* lists *Status Quo* under the category of "Opera" in Beyer's works list (p. 53).

Chapter 10. Beyer's Final Years

1. Letter from Cowell to Olive and Harry Cowell, July 10, 1940, Cowell Papers.

2. Letter from Beyer to Cowell, July 20, 1940, Cowell Papers.

3. Letter from Beyer to Cowell, August 7, 1940, Cowell Papers.

4. Sidney Robertson's tape (transcribed), October 18, 1974, Cowell Papers.

5. This is evident from letters to his parents written on August 3, 1940, August 9, 1940, and August 30, 1940 (Cowell Papers).

6. Letter from Beyer to Cowell, December 5, 1940, Cowell Papers.

7. Cowell to Olive and Harry Cowell, December 20, 1940, Cowell Papers.

8. Letter from Beyer to Cowell, January 4, 1941, Cowell Papers. The two compositions she mentions in this letter—the "movement for winds" and "four movements for strings"—are most likely the Trio for Woodwinds and String Quartet No. 4.

9. Letter from Beyer to Sevitzky, April 17, 1941, Sevitzky Papers.

10. Letter from Beyer to Cowell, January 7[?], 1941, Cowell Papers.

11. See Reynolds, "Informal Autobiography," typescript, Reynolds Papers.

12. Letter from Beyer to Cowell, January 7[?], 1941, Cowell Papers. The friends she alludes to are Bertha Reynolds and the Overstreets (mentioned earlier in the letter).

13. Letter from Beyer to Cowell, January 14, 1941, and postcard from Beyer to Cowell, postmarked January 17, 1941, Cowell Papers.

14. Letter from Cowell to Beyer, January 15, 1941, Cowell Papers.

15. Cowell's financial records, check stubs, Cowell Papers.

16. Letter from Beyer to Cowell, January 15, 1941, Cowell Papers.

17. Letter from Cowell to Sidney Robertson, January 25, 1941.

18. Letter from Beyer to Cowell, February 5, 1941, Cowell Papers. The piece she had finished "for Stokowski" was her Symphonic Movement II.

19. Both of Graham's new pieces were premiered at Bennington College on August 11, 1940, with Cunningham as one of the soloists in *El Penitente*.

20. Letter from Reynolds to Cowell, January 22, 1941, Cowell Papers.

21. Letter from Beyer to Cowell, March 22, 1941, Cowell Papers.

22. Letter from Beyer to Cowell, March 14, 1941, Cowell Papers.

23. Letter from Beyer to Cowell, undated, Cowell Papers.

24. Letter from Beyer to Cowell, April 3, 1941, Cowell Papers.

25. Cowell's datebooks (pocket calendars), Cowell Papers.

26. Letter from Cowell to Beyer, June 3, 1941, Cowell Papers.

27. Letter from Beyer to Cowell, postmarked June 4, 1941, Cowell Papers.

28. On typed page marked 7/11—5-a—, "footnote 7, Johanna Beyer"; in folder labeled

"Sidney Cowell book on Henry Cowell [1944] chapter headings, footnotes [12/19/1975]," Cowell Papers.

29. On January 25, 1988, Cage wrote to John Kennedy: "I remember Johanna very little though I enjoyed her when I was with her"; copy provided by Kennedy.

30. The American Composers Alliance was established in 1937, and the American Music Center was established in 1939. It is unclear who picked up Beyer's manuscripts and where they first went before being stored at the American Music Center. (Just a few years after Beyer's death, the American Music Center's board of directors included Marion Bauer [treasurer], Quincy Porter, Aaron Copland, Harrison Kerr, Ray Green [executive secretary], Otto Luening [chairman], William Schuman, Howard Hanson, and Douglas Moore, among others.) This is the second reference I have found to Beyer's having written something close to one hundred pieces, the other reference being in the letter from Beyer to Cowell, postmarked June 4, 1941, quoted above (n27).

Conclusion

The title of this chapter, "May the Future Be Kind to All Composers," are Johanna Beyer's words to Henry Cowell in a letter dated March 22, 1941 (Cowell Papers).

1. Letter from Paul Price to Ussachevsky, September 21, 1953; letter from Ussachevsky to Price, January 12, 1954, New Music Society Archives Papers.

2. The performance took place on May 11, 1961; see "Concert and Opera Programs."

3. Thanks to Ron Coulter for providing information about the location of Beyer's percussion ensemble manuscripts in the John Cage *Notations* collection at Northwestern University.

4. Amirkhanian, liner notes for the New World Records reissue of the 1750 Arch Street label's recording called "New Music for Electronic and Recorded Media: Women In Electronic Music 1977."

5. The musicians on the 1750 Arch Street recording of *Music of the Spheres* were Donald Buchla, Brenda Hutchinson, Allen Strange, David Morse, and Stephen Ruppenthal, with Robert Shumaker (recording engineer).

6. Boziwick, email communication with the author, February 15, 2013.

7. Letter from William Powell to Frank Campbell, chief of Music Division, New York Public Library, August 9, 1984.

8. Letter from Slonimsky to John Kennedy, after January 24, 1988. Amirkhanian has written: "Slonimsky, who knew of Beyer through Cowell, and who is the most thorough of musical investigators, refused for years to include her in *Baker's Dictionary of Musicians* because he did not have her exact dates of birth and death." See Amirkhanian, "Johanna Magdalena Beyer."

9. This short write-up prior to the November 1988 concerts probably appeared in the *Village Voice*; I found a copy in the Peter Garland Papers, Harry Ransom Center at the University of Texas in Austin. On another occasion Gann referred to Beyer as "obscure but extremely innovative." See Gann, "Subversive Prophet," 208.

10. Rockwell, "Long-Forgotten Works." This sentiment is echoed by the descriptive abstract in the New York Public Library's Finding Aid for the Johanna Magdalena Beyer

scores (1931–1943), JPB 82-77: "The Johanna Magdalena Beyer scores represent the work of a *neglected* woman composer." Emphasis added.

11. Hixon and Hennessee, *Women in Music*, 103. Hixon and Hennessee's sources included Slonimsky's 1984 and 1992 editions of *Baker's Biographical Dictionary*, Cohen's *International Encyclopedia of Women Composers* (1987), and an anthology of flute music by women composers.

12. Emphasis added.

13. For more information on the Frog Peak/Johanna Beyer Project, see http://www.frogpeak.org/fpartists/beyer.lists.html (accessed July 10, 2014). Additional Beyer-related resources are available at http://eamusic.dartmouth.edu/~larry/misc_writings/talks/beyer.index.html (accessed July 10, 2014).

14. Lange, "Reviews." Emphasis added.

Appendix A. Biographical Data

1. Letter from Anett Müller, Stadtarchiv, Stadt Leipzig, to Cordula Jasper (Berlin), August 19, 1997; copy provided by Larry Polansky.

2. According to the *American Druggist and Pharmaceutical Record*, vol. 34 (1899), and the *Druggists' Circular and Chemical Gazette*, vol. 43 (May 1890), a Henry Birch lived at 661 Columbus Avenue and was a member of the Manhattan Pharmaceutical Association.

3. An immigration record for a Marie Brueck shows that she was traveling to Montclair, New Jersey, in 1922; the name Mary [*sic*] Brueck also appeared on Beyer's 1911 ship manifest record.

4. Frida Kastner died on June 10, 1997 in Redding, Connecticut.

SOURCES AND BIBLIOGRAPHY

Primary Sources

Ancestry.com
  New York State Census, 1925
  U.S. Census Records, 1930
  U.S. Census Records, 1940
  U.S. Public Records Index
Avery Library Drawings and Archives, Columbia University, New York
  E. E. Wood Papers
Elmer L. Anderson Library, University of Minnesota, Minneapolis
  Henry Street Settlement School Records, Social Welfare History Archives
Greenwich Village Historical Society, New York
Hargrove Music Library, University of California, Berkeley
  Henry Cowell Correspondence
Harry Ransom Center, University of Texas, Austin
  Peter Garland Papers
Irving S. Gilmore Music Library, Special Collections, Yale University, New Haven, Conn.
  Charles Ives Papers
  Quincy Porter Papers
Library of Congress, Music Division, Washington, D.C.
  Percy Grainger Collection
  Serge Koussevitzky Collection
  Fabien Sevitzky Papers
  Nicolas Slonimsky Collection
  Ruth Crawford Seeger Papers
McHenry Library Special Collections and Archive, University of California, Santa Cruz
  Lou Harrison Papers
New York Historical Society Library
New York Public Library for the Performing Arts, Astor, Lenox, and Tilden Foundations, Music Division
  Johanna Magdalena Beyer Scores
  Henry Cowell Papers

New Music Society Papers
Northwestern University, Evanston, Ill.
John Cage Collection
Percy Grainger Museum, Melbourne, Australia
Percy Grainger Papers
Solomon R. Guggenheim Museum Archives, New York
Guggenheim Foundation Records
Sophia Smith Collection, Smith College, Northampton, Mass.
Bertha Reynolds Papers
Statue of Liberty–Ellis Island Foundation, New York
Ellis Island Records
Tamiment Library and Robert F. Wagner Labor Archive, Bobst Library, New York University, New York
Greenwich House Music School Records
U.S. State Department, Passport Services, Office of Legal Affairs, Washington, D.C.
Xth Olympiade Committee of the Games of Los Angeles, USA (1933)
Games of the Xth Olympiad: Official Report of the 1932 Summer Olympic Games, Los Angeles

Secondary Sources

"Activities of Musicians Here and Afield." *New York Times*, October 22, 1933.

Amirkhanian, Charles. "Johanna Magdalena Beyer: A Discovery Waiting to Happen." In "Johanna Magdalena Beyer: 100th Birthday Commemoration," program notes for Essential Music's two concerts of Beyer's music (1988).

Bauer, Marion. *Twentieth Century Music: How It Developed, How to Listen to It*. New York: Putnam's, 1933.

Beal, Amy C. "'Her Whimsy and Originality Really Amount to Genius': New Biographical Research on Johanna Beyer," *American Music Review* 38, no. 1 (Fall 2008): 1, 4–5, 12–13.

Bick, Sally. "In the Tradition of Dissent: Music at the New School for Social Research, 1926–33." *Journal of the American Musicological Society* 66, no. 1 (Spring 2013): 129–90.

Boland, Marguerite. "Experimentation and Process in the Music of Johanna Beyer." *VivaVoce No. 86, Journal of the Internationaler Arbeitskreis Frau and Musik* (2007), unpaginated.

Boziwick, George. "Henry Cowell at the New York Public Library: A Whole World of Music." *Notes* (September 2000): 46–58.

Carl, Robert. *Modern American Bass*. Robert Black, bass. Liner notes. New World Records 80722-2, 2011, 4.

Cohen, Aaron I. *International Encyclopedia of Women Composers*. New York: Books and Music USA, 1987.

Cohn, Arthur. "Americans in the Fleisher Collection." *Modern Music* 16, no. 2 (January–February 1939): 16–19.

"Composers-Forum Concert." *New York Times*, February 12, 1940.

"Composers' Forum Record." *New York Times*, June 28, 1936.

"The Composers Organize: A Proclamation." *Modern Music* 15, no. 2 (January–February 1938): 92–95.

"Concert at WPA Theatre: Works of Johanna M. Beyer and Walter Helfer Presented." *New York Times*, May 20, 1937.

Copland, Aaron. "Scores and Records." *Modern Music* 16, no. 2 (January–February 1939), 122–25.

Coulter, Ron. "Forgotten Works: Johanna Magdalena Beyer." Unpublished essay, 2013.

Cowell, Henry. "Drums along the Pacific." *Modern Music* 18, no. 1 (November–December 1940): 46–49.

———, ed. *American Composers on American Music: A Symposium*. Stanford, Calif.: Stanford University Press / London: Oxford University Press, 1933.

Crawford, Richard. *America's Musical Life: A History*. New York: Norton, 2001.

de Graaf, Melissa J. "Documenting Music in the New Deal: The New York Composers' Forum Concerts, 1935–1940." PhD diss., Brandeis University, Waltham, Mass., 2005.

———. "Intersection of Gender and Modernism in the Music of Johanna Beyer." *ISAM Newsletter* 33, no. 2 (Spring 2004): 8–9, 15.

———. "'Never Call Us Lady Composers': Gendered Receptions in the New York Composers' Forum, 1935–1940." *American Music* (Fall 2008): 277–308.

———. *The New York Composers' Forum Concerts, 1935–1940*. Rochester, N.Y.: University of Rochester Press, 2013.

Fisher, Marjory M. "Interest Shown in Percussion Music Program." *San Francisco News*, May 8, 1942.

Galván, Gary. "The ABCs of the WPA Music Copying Project and the Fleisher Collection." *American Music* 26, no. 4 (Winter 2008): 514–38.

Gann, Kyle. *American Music in the Twentieth Century*. New York: Schirmer, 1997.

———. "Subversive Prophet: Henry Cowell as Theorist and Critic." In *The Whole World of Music: A Henry Cowell Symposium*, edited by David Nicholls, 171–222. Amsterdam: Harwood Academic, 1997.

Gilbert, Steven E. "'The Ultra-Modern Idiom': A Survey of New Music." *Perspectives of New Music* 12, nos. 1–2 (Autumn 1973–Summer 1974): 282–314.

Glöckler, Ralph Roger. *Mr. Ives und die Vettern vierten Grades*. Berlin: Elfenbein Verlag, 2012.

Gregory, Montgomery. "The Drama of Negro Life." In *The New Negro: Voices of the Harlem Renaissance*, edited by Alain Locke, 153–60. New York: Simon and Schuster, 1925.

Hall, David. "New Music Quarterly Recordings: A Discography." *Association of Recorded Sound Collections* 16, nos. 1–2 (1984): 10–27.

Hicks, Michael. *Henry Cowell: Bohemian*. Urbana: University of Illinois Press, 2002.

———. "The Imprisonment of Henry Cowell." *Journal of the American Musicological Society* 44, no. 1 (Spring 1991): 92–119.

Higgins, Dick, ed. *Essential Cowell: Selected Writings on Music*. Kingston, N.Y.: McPherson, 2000.

Hinkle-Turner, Elizabeth. *Women Composers and Music Technology in the United States*. Burlington, Vt.: Ashgate, 2006.

Hiser, Kelly. "An Enduring Cycle: Revaluing the Life and Music of Johanna Beyer." Master's thesis, University of Miami, 2009.

Hixon, Don L., and Don A. Hennessee, eds. *Women in Music: An Encyclopedic Biobibliography*. Vol. 1, 2nd ed. Metuchen, N.J.: Scarecrow, 1993.

Kennedy, John. "Restless—Endless—Tactless." Liner notes. *Restless—Endless—Tactless: Johanna Beyer and the Birth of American Percussion Music.* New World Records 80711-2, 2011, 2–12.

———. and Larry Polansky. "'Total Eclipse': The Music of Johanna Magdalena Beyer: An Introduction and Preliminary Annotated Checklist." *Musical Quarterly* 80, no. 4 (Winter 1996): 719–78.

Lumsden, Rachel. "Beyond Modernism's Edge: Johanna Beyer's String Quartet No. 2 and Vivian Fine's *The Race of Life.*" PhD diss., City University of New York, 2012.

McCaughey, John. "Unavoidably what may happen is surely a wonderful thing . . . Johanna Beyer's Musical Journeys." Liner notes. *Sticky Melodies: Johanna Beyer*, Astra Chamber Music Society, New World Records 80678-2, 2008, 24–27.

Mead, Rita. "The Amazing Mr. Cowell." *American Music* 1, no. 4 (Winter 1983): 63–89.

———. *Henry Cowell's New Music 1925–1936.* Ann Arbor, Mich.: UMI Research, 1978.

———. "Henry Cowell's New Music Society." *Journal of Musicology* 1, no. 4 (October 1982): 449–63.

Miller, Leta E. "Henry Cowell and John Cage: Intersections and Influences, 1933–1941." *Journal of the American Musicological Society* 59, no. 1 (2006): 47–112.

———, and Rob Collins. "The Cowell-Ives Relationship: A New Look at Cowell's Prison Years." *American Music* 23, no. 4 (Winter 2005): 473–92.

"Music Notes." *New York Times*, May 20, 1936.

Oja, Carol. *Making Music Modern: New York in the 1920s.* New York: Oxford University Press, 2000.

Oteri, Frank J. "Sounds Heard: Restless, Endless, Tactless." *New Music Box Online* (a publication of New Music USA), March 22, 2011.

Pettis, Ashley. "The WPA and the American Composer." *Musical Quarterly* 26, no. 1 (January 1940): 101–12.

Polansky, Larry. "Sticky Melodies . . . : The Choral and Chamber Music of Johanna Magdalena Beyer." Liner notes. *Sticky Melodies: Johanna Beyer*, Astra Chamber Music Society, New World Records 80678-2, 2008, 4–24.

Price, Paul. "Percussion Up-To-Date." *Music Journal* 22, no. 9 (December 1964): 32–33, 67–68.

Rao, Nancy. "American Compositional Theory in the 1930s: Scale and Exoticism in 'The Nature of Melody' by Henry Cowell." *Musical Quarterly* 85, no. 4 (2001): 595–640.

———. "Cowell's Sliding Tone and American Ultra-Modernist Tradition." *American Music* 23, no. 3 (2005): 281–323.

Reese, Kirsten. "Ruhelos: Annäherung an Johanna Magdalena Beyer." *MusikTexte* 81 (December 1999): 6.

Reynolds, Bertha C. *An Uncharted Journey: Fifty Years of Growth in Social Work.* New York: Citadel Press, 1963.

Reynolds, Frank W. *Through the Years to Seventy.* Copyright: Frank W. Reynolds, 1957. Wisconsin State Historical Society.

Rockwell, John. "Long-Forgotten Works of a 30's Avant-Gardist." *New York Times*, November 14, 1988.

Rubin, Joan Shelley. *Songs of Ourselves: The Uses of Poetry in America*. Cambridge, Mass.: Belknap, 2007.

Sachs, Joel. *Henry Cowell: A Man Made of Music*. Oxford: Oxford University Press, 2012.

Schwartz, A. B. Christa. "New Negro Renaissance—'Neger Renaissance': Crossovers between African America and Germany during the Era of the Harlem Renaissance." In *From Black to Schwarz: Cultural Crossovers between African America and Germany*, edited by Maria Diedrich and Jürgen Heinrichs, 49–74. Berlin: LIT Verlag, 2010.

Seeger, Charles. "On Dissonant Counterpoint." *Modern Music* 7, no. 4 (June–July 1930): 25–31.

———. "Tradition and Experiment in (the New) Music." In *Studies in Musicology II, 1929–1979*, edited by Ann M. Pescatello, 39–273. Berkeley: University of California Press, 1994.

Siwe, Tom. "Lou Harrison at the University of Illinois with Tom Siwe." *Percussive Notes* 18, no. 2 (1980): 30–62.

Slonimsky, Nicolas, ed. "Johanna Magdalena Beyer." *Baker's Biographical Dictionary of Musicians*. 8th ed. (1992), 181.

———, ed. *Music Since 1900* (New York: Scribner's, 1971).

Smith, Catherine Parsons. "'A Distinguishing Virility': Feminism and Modernism in American Art Music." In *Cecilia Reclaimed: Perspectives on Gender and Music*, edited by Susan C. Cook, 90–106. Urbana: University of Illinois Press, 1994.

Sokoloff, Nikolai. "Government Gesture an Aid to a National Art." *Musical America* (February 10, 1936): 8.

Spilker, John D. "The Origins of 'Dissonant Counterpoint': Henry Cowell's Unpublished Notebook." *Journal of the Society for American Music* 5, no. 4 (November 2011): 481–533.

Stein, Clarence S. *Toward New Towns for America*. New York: Reinhold, 1957.

Tick, Judith. *Ruth Crawford Seeger: A Composer's Search for American Music*. New York: Oxford University Press, 1997.

———. "Women as Professional Musicians in the United States, 1870–1900. *Anuario Interamericano de Investigacion Musical* 9 (1973): 95–133.

"Two Composers Heard: Forum-Laboratory Offers Ethel Hier and Johanna Beyer." *New York Times*, May 21, 1936.

Tyranny, "Blue" Gene. "88 Keys to Freedom: Segues through the History of American Piano Music." *New Music Box* (Web Magazine for the American Music Center), October 1, 2003. Available at http://www.newmusicbox.org/article.nmbx?id=2219 (accessed July 10, 2014).

Woolfe, Zachary. "Composers." Review of *Bach: Music in the Castle of Heaven*, by John Eliot Gardiner (Knopf, 2013). *New York Times Book Review*, December 8, 2013, 73.

INDEX

AMY C. BEAL is a professor of music at the University of California, Santa Cruz, and the author of *Carla Bley* and *New Music, New Allies: American Experimental Music in West Germany from the Zero Hour to Reunification*.

AMERICAN *Composers*

Lou Harrison
Leta E. Miller and Fredric Lieberman

John Cage
David Nicholls

Dudley Buck
N. Lee Orr

William Grant Still
Catherine Parsons Smith

Rudolf Friml
William Everett

Elliott Carter
James Wierzbicki

Carla Bley
Amy C. Beal

Christian Wolff
Michael Hicks and Christian Asplund

Robert Ashley
Kyle Gann

Alec Wilder
Philip Lambert

Aaron Jay Kernis
Leta E. Miller

Johanna Beyer
Amy C. Beal

The University of Illinois Press
is a founding member of the
Association of American University Presses.

Composed in 9.5/13 Janson Text
with Meta display
by Jim Proefrock
at the University of Illinois Press
Manufactured by Sheridan Books, Inc.

University of Illinois Press
1325 South Oak Street
Champaign, IL 61820-6903
www.press.uillinois.edu